Cambridge Plain Texts

GOLDSMITH

THE GOOD-NATUR'D MAN

GOLDSMITH

THE
GOOD-NATUR'D MAN

CAMBRIDGE
AT THE UNIVERSITY PRESS
1921

CAMBRIDGE UNIVERSITY PRESS

Cambridge, New York, Melbourne, Madrid, Cape Town,
Singapore, São Paulo, Delhi, Mexico City

Cambridge University Press
The Edinburgh Building, Cambridge CB2 8RU, UK

Published in the United States of America by Cambridge University Press, New York

www.cambridge.org
Information on this title: www.cambridge.org/9781107682108

First published 1921
Re-issued 2013

A catalogue record for this publication is available from the British Library

ISBN 978-1-107-68210-8 Paperback

NOTE

AMONG the legacies of a happy genius that touched nothing it did not adorn, OLIVER GOLDSMITH (1728–1774) has left the world two delightful Comedies. But *The Good-Natur'd Man* has never enjoyed, on the stage at any rate, a tithe of the good fortune attendant on his younger sister *She Stoops to Conquer*. We may find the reason for this, if we choose, in the nature of things, and say that our good-natur'd man, Honeywood, was designed—like Goldsmith himself—to be a butt. Garrick took the MS. of the play, doubted its success, made suggestions for improving it, paltered with its sensitive author, and added final injury to supposed insult by forestalling Goldsmith with a rival production, *False Delicacy*, written by Hugh Kelly.

False Delicacy was produced at Drury Lane on Saturday, January 23, 1768, *The Good-Natur'd Man* at the rival house of Covent Garden six nights later. Johnson, Burke, Reynolds and other members of the Literary Club turned up to cheer. The play was saved, as by fire, by the acting of Shuter in the part of 'Croaker'—saved twice before the curtain fell. It ran for ten nights, and the author received something between £350 and £400 by benefit performances on the third, sixth and ninth nights. Kelly's forgotten play brought him more than £700 in book rights alone.

Goldsmith, too, printed, and promptly; in a preface returning 'upon the whole' his thanks to the public for the favourable reception *The Good-Natur'd Man* had met with. The preface ends, as did Dr Johnson's Prologue, spoken on the first night, with a simple claim that the play be judged on its merit. No one can deny a handsome award to the characters of Croaker and Lofty—whose pretence and detection make together one of the finest things in English comedy—or wholesome laughter to the general fun of the plot.

Q.

December, 1920

PROLOGUE

WRITTEN BY DR JOHNSON:

SPOKEN BY MR BENSLEY

PREST by the load of life, the weary mind
Surveys the general toil of human kind;
With cool submission joins the labouring train,
And social sorrow loses half its pain:
Our anxious Bard, without complaint, may share
This bustling season's epidemic care,
Like Cæsar's pilot, dignified by fate,
Tost in one common storm with all the great;
Distrest alike, the statesman and the wit,
When one a Borough courts, and one the Pit.
The busy candidates for power and fame,
Have hopes, and fears, and wishes, just the same;
Disabled both to combat, or to fly,
Must hear all taunts, and hear without reply.
Uncheck'd on both, loud rabbles vent their rage,
As mongrels bay the lion in a cage.
Th' offended burgess hoards his angry tale,
For that blest year when all that vote may rail;
Their schemes of spite the poet's foes dismiss,
Till that glad night, when all that hate may hiss.
This day the powder'd curls and golden coat,
Says swelling Crispin, begg'd a cobbler's vote.
This night, our wit, the pert apprentice cries,
Lies at my feet, I hiss him, and he dies.

The great, 'tis true, can charm th' electing tribe;
The bard may supplicate, but cannot bribe.
Yet judg'd by those, whose voices ne'er were sold,
He feels no want of ill-persuading gold;
But, confident of praise, if praise be due,
Trusts without fear, to merit, and to you.

THE GOOD-NATUR'D MAN

ACT THE FIRST

SCENE: AN APARTMENT IN YOUNG
HONEYWOOD'S HOUSE

Enter SIR WILLIAM HONEYWOOD, JARVIS.

SIR WILL. Good Jarvis, make no apologies for this honest bluntness. Fidelity, like yours, is the best excuse for every freedom.

JARVIS. I can't help being blunt, and being very angry too, when I hear you talk of disinheriting so good, so worthy a young gentleman as your nephew, my master. All the world loves him.

SIR WILL. Say rather, that he loves all the world; that is his fault.

JARVIS. I'm sure there is no part of it more dear to him than you are, though he has not seen you since he was a child.

SIR WILL. What signifies his affection to me, or how can I be proud of a place in a heart where every sharper and coxcomb find an easy entrance?

JARVIS. I grant you that he's rather too good-natured; that he's too much every man's man; that he laughs this minute with one, and cries the next with another; but whose instructions may he thank for all this?

SIR WILL. Not mine, sure? My letters to him during my employment in Italy, taught him only that philosophy which might prevent, not defend his errors.

JARVIS. Faith, begging your honour's pardon, I'm sorry they taught him any philosophy at all; it has only served to spoil him. This same philosophy is a good horse in the stable, but an arrant jade on a journey. For my own part, whenever I hear him mention the name on't, I'm always sure he's going to play the fool.

SIR WILL. Don't let us ascribe his faults to his philosophy, I entreat you. No, Jarvis, his good nature arises rather from his fears of offending the importunate, than his desire of making the deserving happy.

JARVIS. What it rises from, I don't know. But, to be sure, everybody has it, that asks it.

SIR WILL. Ay, or that does not ask it. I have been now for some time a concealed spectator of his follies, and find them as boundless as his dissipation.

JARVIS. And yet, faith, he has some fine name or other for them all. He calls his extravagance, generosity; and his trusting everybody, universal benevolence. It was but last week he went security for a fellow whose face he scarce knew, and that he called an act of exalted mu—mu—munificence; ay, that was the name he gave it.

SIR WILL. And upon that I proceed, as my last effort, though with very little hopes to reclaim him. That very fellow has just absconded, and I have taken up the security. Now, my intention is to involve him in fictitious distress, before he has plunged himself into real calamity. To arrest him for that very debt, to clap an officer upon him, and then let him see which of his friends will come to his relief.

JARVIS. Well, if I could but any way see him thoroughly vexed, every groan of his would be music to me; yet, faith, I believe it impossible. I have tried to fret him myself every morning these three years; but, instead of being angry, he sits as calmly to hear me scold, as he does to his hair-dresser.

Sir Will. We must try him once more, however, and I'll go this instant to put my scheme into execution; and I don't despair of succeeding, as, by your means, I can have frequent opportunities of being about him, without being known. What a pity it is, Jarvis, that any man's good-will to others should produce so much neglect of himself, as to require correction. Yet, we must touch his weaknesses with a delicate hand. There are some faults so nearly allied to excellence, that we can scarce weed out the vice without eradicating the virtue. [*Exit.*

Jarvis. Well, go thy ways, Sir William Honeywood. It is not without reason that the world allows thee to be the best of men. But here comes his hopeful nephew; the strange good-natur'd, foolish, open-hearted—And yet, all his faults were such that one loves him still the better for them.

Enter Honeywood.

Honeyw. Well, Jarvis, what messages from my friends this morning?

Jarvis. You have no friends.

Honeyw. Well; from my acquaintance then?

Jarvis (*pulling out bills*). A few of our usual cards of compliment, that's all. This bill from your tailor; this from your mercer; and this from the little broker in Crooked-lane. He says he has been at a great deal of trouble to get back the money you borrowed.

Honeyw. That I don't know; but I'm sure we were at a great deal of trouble in getting him to lend it.

Jarvis. He has lost all patience.

Honeyw. Then he has lost a very good thing.

Jarvis. There's that ten guineas you were sending to the poor gentleman and his children in the Fleet. I believe that would stop his mouth, for a while at least.

HONEYW. Ay, Jarvis, but what will fill their mouths in the mean time? Must I be cruel because he happens to be importunate; and, to relieve his avarice, leave them to insupportable distress?

JARVIS. 'Sdeath! Sir, the question now is how to relieve yourself. Yourself—Haven't I reason to be out of my senses, when I see things going on at sixes and sevens?

HONEYW. Whatever reason you may have for being out of your senses, I hope you'll allow that I'm not quite unreasonable for continuing in mine.

JARVIS. You're the only man alive in your present situation that could do so—Everything upon the waste. There's Miss Richland and her fine fortune gone already, and upon the point of being given to your rival.

HONEYW. I'm no man's rival.

JARVIS. Your uncle in Italy preparing to disinherit you; your own fortune almost spent; and nothing but pressing creditors, false friends, and a pack of drunken servants that your kindness has made unfit for any other family.

HONEYW. Then they have the more occasion for being in mine.

JARVIS. Soh! What will you have done with him that I caught stealing your plate in the pantry? In the fact; I caught him in the fact.

HONEYW. In the fact! If so, I really think that we should pay him his wages, and turn him off.

JARVIS. He shall be turn'd off at Tyburn, the dog; we'll hang him, if it be only to frighten the rest of the family.

HONEYW. No, Jarvis: it's enough that we have lost what he has stolen, let us not add to it the loss of a fellow-creature!

JARVIS. Very fine; well, here was the footman just now, to complain of the butler; he says he does most work, and ought to have most wages.

HONEYW. That's but just; though perhaps, here comes the butler to complain of the footman.

JARVIS. Ay, it's the way with them all, from the scullion to the privy-counsellor. If they have a bad master, they keep quarrelling with him; if they have a good master, they keep quarrelling with one another.

Enter BUTLER, *drunk.*

BUTLER. Sir, I'll not stay in the family with Jonathan; you must part with him, or part with me, that's the ex-ex-exposition of the matter, sir.

HONEYW. Full and explicit enough. But what's his fault, good Philip?

BUTLER. Sir, he's given to drinking, sir, and I shall have my morals corrupted, by keeping such company.

HONEYW. Ha! Ha! He has such a diverting way—

JARVIS. O quite amusing!

BUTLER. I find my wines a-going, sir; and liquors don't go without mouths, sir; I hate a drunkard, sir!

HONEYW. Well, well, Philip, I'll hear you upon that another time, so go to bed now.

JARVIS. To bed! Let him go to the devil!

BUTLER. Begging your honour's pardon, and begging your pardon master Jarvis, I'll not go to bed, nor to the devil neither. I have enough to do to mind my cellar. I forgot, your honour, Mr Croaker is below. I came on purpose to tell you.

HONEYW. Why didn't you show him up, blockhead?

BUTLER. Show him up, sir? With all my heart, sir. Up or down, all's one to me. [*Exit.*

JARVIS. Ay, we have one or other of that family in this house from morning till night. He comes on the old affair, I suppose. The match between his son, that's just returned from Paris, and Miss Richland, the young lady he's guardian to.

HONEYW. Perhaps so. Mr Croaker, knowing my friendship for the young lady, has got it into his head that I can persuade her to what I please.

JARVIS. Ah! If you loved yourself but half as well as she loves you, we should soon see a marriage that would set all things to rights again.

HONEYW. Love me! Sure, Jarvis, you dream. No, no; her intimacy with me never amounted to more than friendship—mere friendship. That she is the most lovely woman that ever warmed the human heart with desire, I own. But never let me harbour a thought of making her unhappy, by a connection with one so unworthy her merits as I am. No, Jarvis, it shall be my study to serve her, even in spite of my wishes; and to secure her happiness, though it destroys my own.

JARVIS. Was ever the like! I want patience.

HONEYW. Besides, Jarvis, though I could obtain Miss Richland's consent, do you think I could succeed with her guardian, or Mrs Croaker his wife; who, though both very fine in their way, are yet a little opposite in their dispositions, you know.

JARVIS. Opposite enough, Heaven knows; the very reverse of each other; she all laugh and no joke; he always complaining, and never sorrowful; a fretful poor soul that has a new distress for every hour in the four-and-twenty—

HONEYW. Hush, hush, he's coming up, he'll hear you.

JARVIS. One whose voice is a passing bell—

HONEYW. Well, well, go, do.

JARVIS. A raven that bodes nothing but mischief; a coffin and cross bones; a bundle of rue; a sprig of deadly night shade; a— (*Honeywood stopping his mouth at last, pushes him off.*)   [*Exit* JARVIS.

HONEYW. I must own my old monitor is not entirely wrong. There is something in my friend Croaker's conversation that quite depresses me. His very mirth is an antidote to all gaiety, and his appearance has a stronger effect on my spirits than an undertaker's shop.—Mr Croaker, this is such a satisfaction—

Enter CROAKER.

CROAKER. A pleasant morning to Mr Honeywood, and many of them. How is this! You look most shockingly to-day, my dear friend. I hope this weather does not affect your spirits. To be sure, if this weather continues—I say nothing—But God send we be all better this day three months.

HONEYW. I heartily concur in the wish, though I own not in your apprehensions.

CROAKER. May be not! Indeed what signifies what weather we have in a country going to ruin like ours? Taxes rising and trade falling. Money flying out of the kingdom and Jesuits swarming into it. I know at this time no less than a hundred and twenty-seven Jesuits between Charing-cross and Temple-bar.

HONEYW. The Jesuits will scarce pervert you or me, I should hope.

CROAKER. May be not. Indeed what signifies whom they pervert in a country that has scarce any religion to lose? I'm only afraid for our wives and daughters.

HONEYW. I have no apprehensions for the ladies, I assure you.

CROAKER. May be not. Indeed what signifies whether they be perverted or no? The women in my time were good for something. I have seen a lady dressed from top to toe in her own manufactures formerly. But now-a-days, the devil a thing of their own manufactures about them, except their faces.

HONEYW. But, however these faults may be practised abroad, you don't find them at home, either with Mrs Croaker, Olivia or Miss Richland.

CROAKER. The best of them will never be canoniz'd for a saint when she's dead. By the bye, my dear friend, I don't find this match between Miss Richland and my son much relish'd, either by one side or t'other.

HONEYW. I thought otherwise.

CROAKER. Ah, Mr Honeywood, a little of your fine serious advice to the young lady might go far: I know she has a very exalted opinion of your understanding.

HONEYW. But would not that be usurping an authority that more properly belongs to yourself?

CROAKER. My dear friend, you know but little of my authority at home. People think, indeed, because they see me come out in a morning thus, with a pleasant face, and to make my friends merry, that all's well within. But I have cares that would break a heart of stone. My wife has so encroach'd upon every one of my privileges, that I'm now no more than a mere lodger in my own house!

HONEYW. But a little spirit exerted on your side might perhaps restore your authority.

CROAKER. No, though I had the spirit of a lion! I do rouse sometimes. But what then! Always haggling and haggling. A man is tired of getting the better before his wife is tired of losing the victory.

HONEYW. It's a melancholy consideration indeed, that our chief comforts often produce our greatest anxieties, and that an increase of our possessions is but an inlet to new disquietudes.

CROAKER. Ah, my dear friend, these were the very words of poor Dick Doleful to me not a week before he made away with himself. Indeed, Mr Honeywood, I never see you but you put me in mind of poor—Dick. Ah, there was merit neglected for you! and so true a friend! we lov'd each other for thirty years, and yet he never asked me to lend him a single farthing!

HONEYW. Pray what could induce him to commit so rash an action at last?

CROAKER. I don't know, some people were malicious enough to say it was keeping company with me; because we used to meet now and then and open our hearts to each other. To be sure I lov'd to hear him talk, and he lov'd to hear me talk; poor dear Dick. He used to say that Croaker rhymed to joker; and so we used to laugh—Poor Dick. (*Going to cry.*)

HONEYW. His fate affects me.

CROAKER. Ay, he grew sick of this miserable life, where we do nothing but eat and grow hungry, dress and undress, get up and lie down; while reason, that should watch like a nurse by our side, falls as fast asleep as we do.

HONEYW. To say truth, if we compare that part of life which is to come, by that which we have past, the prospect is hideous.

CROAKER. Life at the greatest and best is but a froward child, that must be humour'd and coax'd a little till it falls asleep, and then all the care is over.

HONEYW. Very true, sir, nothing can exceed the vanity of our existence, but the folly of our pursuits. We wept when we came into the world, and every day tells us why.

CROAKER. Ah, my dear friend, it is a perfect satisfaction to be miserable with you. My son Leontine shan't lose the benefit of such fine conversation. I'll just step home for him. I am willing to shew him so much seriousness in one scarce older than himself—And what if I bring my last letter to the Gazetteer on the increase and progress of earthquakes?

It will amuse us, I promise you. I there prove how the late earthquake is coming round to pay us another visit from London to Lisbon, from Lisbon to the Canary Islands, from the Canary Islands to Palmyra, from Palmyra to Constantinople, and so from Constantinople back to London again.

[*Exit.*

HONEYW. Poor Croaker! His situation deserves the utmost pity. I shall scarce recover my spirits these three days. Sure, to live upon such terms is worse than death itself. And yet, when I consider my own situation, a broken fortune, a hopeless passion, friends in distress; the wish but not the power to serve them—— (*pausing and sighing*).

Enter BUTLER.

BUTLER. More company below, sir; Mrs Croaker and Miss Richland; shall I show them up? But they're showing up themselves.   [*Exit.*

Enter MRS CROAKER *and* MISS RICHLAND.

MISS RICH. You're always in such spirits.

MRS CROAKER. We have just come, my dear Honeywood, from the auction. There was the old deaf dowager, as usual, bidding like a fury against herself. And then so curious in antiques! Herself the most genuine piece of antiquity in the whole collection!

HONEYW. Excuse me, ladies, if some uneasiness from friendship makes me unfit to share in this good humour: I know you'll pardon me.

MRS CROAKER. I vow he seems as melancholy as if he had taken a dose of my husband this morning. Well, if Richland here can pardon you, I must.

MISS RICH. You would seem to insinuate, madam, that I have particular reasons for being dispos'd to refuse it.

Mrs Croaker. Whatever I insinuate, my dear, don't be so ready to wish an explanation.

Miss Rich. I own I should be sorry Mr Honeywood's long friendship and mine should be misunderstood.

Honeyw. There's no answering for others, madam. But I hope you'll never find me presuming to offer more than the most delicate friendship may readily allow.

Miss Rich. And I shall be prouder of such a tribute from you than the most passionate professions from others.

Honeyw. My own sentiments, madam: friendship is a disinterested commerce between equals; love, an abject intercourse between tyrants and slaves.

Miss Rich. And, without a compliment, I know none more disinterested or more capable of friendship than Mr Honeywood.

Mrs Croaker. And indeed I know nobody that has more friends, at least among the ladies. Miss Fruzz, Miss Oddbody and Miss Winterbottom, praise him in all companies. As for Miss Biddy Bundle, she's his professed admirer.

Miss Rich. Indeed! an admirer! I did not know, sir, you were such a favourite there. But is she seriously so handsome? Is she the mighty thing talk'd of?

Honeyw. The town, madam, seldom begins to praise a lady's beauty, till she's beginning to lose it! (*Smiling.*)

Mrs Croaker. But she's resolved never to lose it, it seems. For as her natural face decays, her skill improves in making the artificial one. Well, nothing diverts me more than one of those fine old dressy things, who thinks to conceal her age, by everywhere exposing her person; sticking herself up in the front of a side-box; trailing through a minuet at Almack's; and then, in the public gardens; looking for all the world like one of the painted ruins of the place.

Honeyw. Every age has its admirers, ladies. While you,

perhaps, are trading among the warmer climates of youth, there ought to be some to carry on a useful commerce in the frozen latitudes beyond fifty.

MISS RICH. But then the mortifications they must suffer before they can be fitted out for traffic. I have seen one of them fret a whole morning at her hair-dresser, when all the fault was her face.

HONEYW. And yet I'll engage has carried that face at last to a very good market. This good-natur'd town, madam, has husbands, like spectacles, to fit every age, from fifteen to fourscore.

MRS CROAKER. Well, you're a dear good-natur'd creature. But you know you're engaged with us this morning upon a strolling party. I want to shew Olivia the town, and the things; I believe I shall have business for you for the whole day.

HONEYW. I am sorry, madam, I have an appointment with Mr Croaker, which it is impossible to put off.

MRS CROAKER. What! with my husband! Then I'm resolved to take no refusal. Nay, I protest you must. You know I never laugh so much as with you.

HONEYW. Why, if I must, I must. I'll swear you have put me into such spirits. Well, do you find jest, and I'll find laugh, I promise you. We'll wait for the chariot in the next room.   [*Exeunt.*

Enter LEONTINE *and* OLIVIA.

LEONT. There they go, thoughtless and happy. My dearest Olivia, what would I give to see you capable of sharing in their amusements, and as cheerful as they are.

OLIVIA. How, my Leontine, how can I be cheerful, when I have so many terrors to oppress me? The fear of being detected by this family, and the apprehensions of a censuring world, when I must be detected—

LEONT. The world! my love, what can it say? At worst it can only say that, being compelled by a mercenary guardian to embrace a life you disliked, you formed a resolution of flying with the man of your choice; that you confided in his honour, and took refuge in my father's house; the only one where your's could remain without censure.

OLIVIA. But consider, Leontine, your disobedience and my indiscretion: your being sent to France to bring home a sister; and, instead of a sister, bringing home—

LEONT. One dearer than a thousand sisters. One that I am convinc'd will be equally dear to the rest of the family, when she comes to be known.

OLIVIA. And that, I fear, will shortly be.

LEONT. Impossible, till we ourselves think proper to make the discovery. My sister, you know, has been with her aunt, at Lyons, since she was a child, and you find every creature in the family takes you for her.

OLIVIA. But mayn't she write, mayn't her aunt write?

LEONT. Her aunt scarce ever writes, and all my sister's letters are directed to me.

OLIVIA. But won't your refusing Miss Richland, for whom you know the old gentleman intends you, create a suspicion?

LEONT. There, there's my master-stroke. I have resolved not to refuse her; nay, an hour hence I have consented to go with my father, to make her an offer of my heart and fortune.

OLIVIA. Your heart and fortune!

LEONT. Don't be alarm'd, my dearest. Can Olivia think so meanly of my honour, or my love, as to suppose I could ever hope for happiness from any but her? No, my Olivia, neither the force, nor, permit me to add, the delicacy of my passion, leave any room to suspect me. I only offer Miss Richland a heart I am convinced she will refuse; as I am confidant that, without knowing it, her affections are fixed upon Mr Honeywood.

OLIVIA. Mr Honeywood! You'll excuse my apprehensions; but when your merits come to be put in the balance—

LEONT. You view them with too much partiality. However, by making this offer, I show a seeming compliance with my father's commands; and perhaps, upon her refusal, I may have his consent to choose for myself.

OLIVIA. Well, I submit. And yet, my Leontine, I own, I shall envy her even your pretended addresses. I consider every look, every expression of your esteem, as due only to me. This is folly, perhaps: I allow it; but it is natural to suppose, that merit which has made an impression on one's own heart, may be powerful over that of another.

LEONT. Don't, my life's treasure, don't let us make imaginary evils, when you know we have so many real ones to encounter. At worst, you know, if Miss Richland should consent, or my father refuse his pardon, it can but end in a trip to Scotland; and— —

Enter CROAKER.

CROAKER. Where have you been, boy? I have been seeking you. My friend Honeywood here, has been saying such comfortable things. Ah! he's an example indeed. Where is he? I left him here.

LEONT. Sir, I believe you may see him, and hear him, too, in the next room: he's preparing to go out with the ladies.

CROAKER. Good gracious, can I believe my eyes or my ears! I'm struck dumb with his vivacity, and stunn'd with the loudness of his laugh. Was there ever such a transformation! (*A laugh behind the scenes, Croaker mimics it.*) Ha! ha! ha! there it goes: a plague take their balderdash; yet

I could expect nothing less, when my precious wife was of the party. On my conscience, I believe she could spread a horse-laugh through the pews of a tabernacle.

LEONT. Since you find so many objections to a wife, sir, how can you be so earnest in recommending one to me?

CROAKER. I have told you, and tell you again, boy, that Miss Richland's fortune must not go out of the family; one may find comfort in the money, whatever one does in the wife.

LEONT. But, sir, though, in obedience to your desire, I am ready to marry her, it may be possible she has no inclination to me.

CROAKER. I'll tell you once for all how it stands. A good part of Miss Richland's large fortune consists in a claim upon government, which my good friend Mr Lofty, assures me the Treasury will allow. One half of this she is to forfeit, by her father's will, in case she refuses to marry you. So, if she rejects you, we seize half her fortune; if she accepts you, we seize the whole, and a fine girl into the bargain.

LEONT. But, sir, if you will but listen to reason—

CROAKER. Come, then, produce your reasons. I tell you I'm fixed, determined, so now produce your reasons. When I'm determined, I always listen to reason, because it can then do no harm.

LEONT. You have alleged that a mutual choice was the first requisite in matrimonial happiness.

CROAKER. Well, and you have both of you a mutual choice. She has her choice—to marry you, or lose half her fortune; and you have your choice—to marry her, or pack out of doors without any fortune at all.

LEONT. An only son, sir, might expect more indulgence.

CROAKER. An only father, sir, might expect more obedience; besides, has not your sister here, that never disobliged me in her life, as good a right as you? He's a sad dog, Livy, my dear, and would take all from you. But he shan't, I tell you he shan't, for you shall have your share.

OLIVIA. Dear sir, I wish you'd be convinced that I can never be happy in any addition to my fortune, which is taken from his.

CROAKER. Well, well, it's a good child, so say no more, but come with me, and we shall see something that will give us a great deal of pleasure, I promise you; old Ruggins, the curry-comb-maker, lying in state; I'm told he makes a very handsome corpse, and becomes his coffin prodigiously. He was an intimate friend of mine, and these are friendly things we ought to do for each other.   *[Exeunt.*

END OF THE FIRST ACT

ACT THE SECOND

Miss Richland, Garnet.

Miss Rich. Olivia not his sister? Olivia not Leontine's sister? You amaze me!

Gar. No more his sister than I am; I had it all from his own servant; I can get anything from that quarter.

Miss Rich. But how? Tell me again, Garnet.

Gar. Why, madam, as I told you before, instead of going to Lyons to bring home his sister, who has been there with her aunt these ten years, he never went further than Paris; there he saw and fell in love with this young lady; by the bye, of a prodigious family.

Miss Rich. And brought her home to my guardian, as his daughter?

Gar. Yes, and daughter she will be. If he don't consent to their marriage, they talk of trying what a Scotch parson can do.

Miss Rich. Well, I own they have deceived me—And so demurely as Olivia carried it, too!—Would you believe it, Garnet, I told her all my secrets; and yet the sly cheat concealed all this from me?

Gar. And, upon my word, Madam, I don't much blame her; she was loath to trust one with her secrets, that was so very bad at keeping her own.

Miss Rich. But, to add to their deceit, the young gentleman, it seems, pretends to make me serious proposals. My guardian and he are to be here presently, to open the affair

G.   2 in form. You know I am to lose half my fortune if I refuse him.

GAR. Yet, what can you do? For being, as you are, in love with Mr Honeywood, madam—

MISS RICH. How! idiot! what do you mean? In love with Mr Honeywood! Is this to provoke me?

GAR. That is, madam, in friendship with him; I meant nothing more than friendship, as I hope to be married; nothing more.

MISS RICH. Well, no more of this! As to my guardian, and his son, they shall find me prepared to receive them; I'm resolved to accept their proposal with seeming pleasure, to mortify them by compliance, and to throw the refusal at last upon them.

GAR. Delicious! and that will secure your whole fortune to yourself. Well, who could have thought so innocent a face could cover so much cuteness!

MISS RICH. Why, girl, I only oppose my prudence to their cunning, and practise a lesson they have taught me against themselves.

GAR. Then you're likely not long to want employment, for here they come, and in close conference!

Enter CROAKER, LEONTINE.

LEONT. Excuse me, sir, if I seem to hesitate upon the point of putting the lady so important a question.

CROAKER. Lord! good sir, moderate your fears; you're so plaguy shy, that one would think you had changed sexes. I tell you we must have the half or the whole. Come, let me see with what spirit you begin? Well, why don't you? Eh! What? Well then—I must, it seems—Miss Richland, my dear, I believe you guess at our business; an affair which my son here comes to open, that nearly concerns your happiness.

MISS RICH. Sir, I should be ungrateful not to be pleased with anything that comes recommended by you.

CROAKER. How, boy, could you desire a finer opening? Why don't you begin, I say? (*To Leont.*)

LEONT. 'Tis true, madam, my father, madam, has some intentions—hem—of explaining an affair—which—himself —can best explain, madam.

CROAKER. Yes, my dear; it comes entirely from my son; it's all a request of his own, madam. And I will permit him to make the best of it.

LEONT. The whole affair is only this, madam; my father has a proposal to make, which he insists none but himself shall deliver.

CROAKER. My mind misgives me, the fellow will never be brought on. (*Aside.*)—In short, madam, you see before you one that loves you; one whose whole happiness is all in you.

MISS RICH. I never had any doubts of your regard, sir, and I hope you can have none of my duty.

CROAKER. That's not the thing, my little sweeting, my love! No, no, another guess lover than I; there he stands, madam; his very looks declare the force of his passion!—Call up a look, you dog—But then, had you seen him, as I have, weeping, speaking soliloquies and blank verse, sometimes melancholy, and sometimes absent—

MISS RICH. I fear, sir, he's absent now; or such a declaration would have come most properly from himself.

CROAKER. Himself! madam! he would die before he could make such a confession; and if he had not a channel for his passion through me, it would ere now have drowned his understanding.

MISS RICH. I must grant, sir, there are attractions in

modest diffidence, above the force of words. A silent address is the genuine eloquence of sincerity.

CROAKER. Madam, he has forgot to speak any other language; silence is become his mother tongue.

MISS RICH. And it must be confessed, sir, it speaks very powerfully in his favour. And yet, I shall be thought too forward in making such a confession; shan't I, Mr Leontine?

LEONT. Confusion! my reserve will undo me. But, if modesty attracts her, impudence may disgust her. I'll try. (*Aside.*)—Don't imagine from my silence, madam, that I want a due sense of the honour and happiness intended me. My father, madam, tells me your humble servant is not totally indifferent to you. He admires you; I adore you; and when we come together, upon my soul I believe we shall be the happiest couple in all St James's!

MISS RICH. If I could flatter myself you thought as you speak, sir——

LEONT. Doubt my sincerity, madam? By your dear self I swear. Ask the brave if they desire glory; ask cowards if they covet safety——

CROAKER. Well, well, no more questions about it.

LEONT. Ask the sick if they long for health, ask misers if they love money, ask——

CROAKER. Ask a fool if he can talk nonsense! What's come over the boy? What signifies asking, when there's not a soul to give you an answer? If you would ask to the purpose, ask this lady's consent to make you happy.

MISS RICH. Why, indeed, sir, his uncommon ardour almost compels me, forces me, to comply. And yet I'm afraid he'll despise a conquest gained with too much ease; won't you, Mr Leontine?

LEONT. Confusion! (*Aside.*)—O, by no means, madam, by no means. And yet, madam, you talked of force. There is nothing I would avoid so much as compulsion in a thing of this kind. No, madam, I will still be generous, and leave you at liberty to refuse.

CROAKER. But I tell you, sir, the lady is not at liberty. It's a match. You see she says nothing. Silence gives consent.

LEONT. But, sir, she talked of force. Consider, sir, the cruelty of constraining her inclinations.

CROAKER. But I say there's no cruelty. Don't you know, blockhead, that girls have always a roundabout way of saying yes before company? So get you both gone together into the next room, and hang him that interrupts the tender explanation. Get you gone, I say; I'll not hear a word.

LEONT. But, sir, I must beg leave to insist——

CROAKER. Get off, you puppy, or I'll beg leave to insist upon knocking you down. Stupid whelp! But I don't wonder, the boy takes entirely after his mother!

[*Exeunt* MISS RICH. *and* LEONT.

Enter MRS CROAKER.

MRS CROAKER. Mr Croaker, I bring you something, my dear, that I believe will make you smile.

CROAKER. I'll hold you a guinea of that, my dear.

MRS CROAKER. A letter; and, as I knew the hand, I ventured to open it!

CROAKER. And how can you expect your breaking open my letters should give me pleasure?

MRS CROAKER. Poo, it's from your sister at Lyons, and contains good news: read it.

CROAKER. What a Frenchified cover is here! That sister of mine has some good qualities, but I could never teach her to fold a letter.

MRS CROAKER. Fold a fiddlestick! Read what it contains.

CROAKER (*reading*).

DEAR NICK,

An English gentleman, of large fortune, has for some time made private, though honourable proposals to your daughter Olivia. They love each other tenderly, and I find she has consented, without letting any of the family know, to crown his addresses. As such good offers don't come every day, your own good sense, his large fortune, and family considerations, will induce you to forgive her.

Yours ever,

RACHEL CROAKER.

My daughter, Olivia, privately contracted to a man of large fortune! This is good news indeed! My heart never foretold me of this. And yet, how slily the little baggage has carried it since she came home. Not a word on't to the old ones for the world. Yet, I thought I saw something she wanted to conceal.

MRS CROAKER. Well, if they have concealed their amour, they shan't conceal their wedding; that shall be public, I'm resolved.

CROAKER. I tell thee, woman, the wedding is the most foolish part of the ceremony. I can never get this woman to think of the more serious part of the nuptial engagement.

MRS CROAKER. What, would you have me think of their funeral? But come, tell me, my dear, don't you owe more to me than you care to confess? Would you have ever been known to Mr Lofty, who has undertaken Miss Richland's claim at the Treasury, but for me? Who was it first made him an acquaintance at Lady Shabbaroon's rout? Who got him to promise us his interest? Is not he a backstairs favourite, one that can do what he pleases with those that do what they please? Isn't he an acquaintance that all your groaning and lamentations could never have got us?

CROAKER. He is a man of importance, I grant you. And yet, what amazes me is, that while he is giving away places to all the world, he can't get one for himself.

MRS CROAKER. That perhaps may be owing to his nicety. Great men are not easily satisfied!

Enter FRENCH SERVANT.

SERVANT. An expresse from Monsieur Lofty. He vil be vait upon your honours instammant. He be only giving four five instruction, read two tree memorial, call upon von ambassadeur! He vil be vid you in one tree minutes.

MRS CROAKER. You see now, my dear. What an extensive department! Well, friend, let your master know, that we are extremely honoured by this honour. Was there anything ever in a higher style of breeding! All messages among the great are now done by express.

CROAKER. To be sure, no man does little things with more solemnity, or claims more respect than he. But he's in the right on't. In our bad world, respect is given, where respect is claimed.

MRS CROAKER. Never mind the world, my dear; you were never in a pleasanter place in your life. Let us now think of receiving him with proper respect (*a loud rapping at the door*) and there he is, by the thundering rap.

CROAKER. Ay, verily, there he is; as close upon the heels of his own express, as an endorsement upon the back of a bill. Well, I'll leave you to receive him, whilst I go to chide my little Olivia for intending to steal a marriage without mine or her aunt's consent. I must seem to be angry, or she, too, may begin to despise my authority. [*Exit.*

Enter LOFTY, *speaking to his servant.*

LOFTY. And if the Venetian Ambassador, or that teasing creature the Marquis, should call, I'm not at home. Dam'me, I'll be pack-horse to none of them! My dear madam, I have just snatched a moment—And if the expresses to his Grace be ready, let them be sent off; they're of importance. Madam, I ask a thousand pardons!

MRS CROAKER. Sir, this honour——

LOFTY. And, Dubardieu! If the person calls about the commission, let him know that it is made out. As for Lord Cumbercourt's stale request, it can keep cold: you understand me. Madam, I ask ten thousand pardons!

MRS CROAKER. Sir, this honour——

LOFTY. And, Dubardieu! If the man comes from the Cornish borough, you must do him; you must do him, I say! Madam, I ask ten thousand pardons! And if the Russian—Ambassador calls: but he will scarce call to-day, I believe. And now, madam, I have just got time to express my happiness in having the honour of being permitted to profess myself your most obedient humble servant!

MRS CROAKER. Sir, the happiness and honour are all mine; and yet, I'm only robbing the public while I detain you.

LOFTY. Sink the public, madam, when the fair are to be attended. Ah, could all my hours be so charmingly devoted! Sincerely, don't you pity us poor creatures in affairs? Thus it is eternally; solicited for places here, teased for pensions there, and courted everywhere. I know you pity me. Yes, I see you do!

MRS CROAKER. Excuse me, sir. Toils of empires pleasures are, as Waller says.

LOFTY. Waller, Waller; is he of the House?

MRS CROAKER. The modern poet of that name, sir.

LOFTY. Oh, a modern! We men of business despise the moderns; and as for the ancients, we have no time to read them. Poetry is a pretty thing enough for our wives and daughters; but not for us. Why now, here I stand that know nothing of books. I say, madam, I know nothing of books; and yet, I believe, upon a land carriage fishery, a stamp act, or a jag-hire, I can talk my two hours without feeling the want of them!

MRS CROAKER. The world is no stranger to Mr Lofty's eminence in every capacity!

LOFTY. I vow to Gad, madam, you make me blush. I'm nothing, nothing, nothing in the world; a mere obscure gentleman! To be sure, indeed, one or two of the present ministers are pleased to represent me as a formidable man. I know they are pleased to bespatter me at all their little dirty levées. Yet, upon my soul, I wonder what they see in me to treat me so! Measures, not men, have always been my mark; and I vow, by all that's honourable, my resentment has never done the men, as mere men, any manner of harm— That is, as mere men.

MRS CROAKER. What importance, and yet what modesty!

LOFTY. Oh, if you talk of modesty, madam! There, I own, I'm accessible to praise: modesty is my foible: it was so the Duke of Brentford used to say of me. I love Jack Lofty, he used to say: no man has a finer knowledge of things; quite a man of information; and when he speaks upon his legs, by the lord, he's prodigious, he scouts them; and yet all men have their faults; too much modesty is his, says his Grace.

MRS CROAKER. And yet, I dare say, you don't want assurance when you come to solicit for your friends.

LOFTY. O, there indeed I'm in bronze. A-propos, I have just been mentioning Miss Richland's case to a certain personage; we must name no names. When I ask, I am not to be put off, madam! No, no, I take my friend by the button. A fine girl, sir; great justice in her case. A friend of mine. Borough interest. Business must be done, Mr Secretary. I say, Mr Secretary, her business must be done, sir. That's my way, madam!

MRS CROAKER. Bless me! you said all this to the Secretary of State, did you?

LOFTY. I did not say the Secretary, did I? Well, curse it, since you have found me out, I will not deny it. It was to the Secretary!

MRS CROAKER. This was going to the fountain-head at once, not applying to the understrappers, as Mr Honeywood would have had us.

LOFTY. Honeywood! he! he! He was, indeed, a fine solicitor. I suppose you have heard what has just happened to him?

MRS CROAKER. Poor dear man! no accident, I hope!

LOFTY. Undone, madam, that's all. His creditors have taken him into custody. A prisoner in his own house!

MRS CROAKER. A prisoner in his own house! How! At this very time! I'm quite unhappy for him.

LOFTY. Why, so am I! The man, to be sure, was immensely good-natur'd. But then, I could never find that he had anything in him.

MRS CROAKER. His manner, to be sure, was excessive harmless; some, indeed, thought it a little dull. For my part, I always concealed my opinion.

LOFTY. It can't be concealed, madam; the man was dull, dull as the last new comedy! A poor impracticable creature! I tried once or twice to know if he was fit for business; but he had scarce talents to be groom-porter to an orange barrow!

MRS CROAKER. How differently does Miss Richland think of him! For, I believe, with all his faults, she loves him.

LOFTY. Loves him! Does she? You should cure her of that, by all means. Let me see, what if she were sent to him this instant, in his present doleful situation? My life for it, that works her cure! Distress is a perfect antidote to love. Suppose we join her in the next room? Miss Richland is a fine girl, has a fine fortune, and must not be thrown away. Upon my honour, madam, I have a regard for Miss Richland; and, rather than she should be thrown away, I should think it no indignity to marry her myself!   [*Exeunt.*

Enter OLIVIA *and* LEONTINE.

LEONT. And yet, trust me, Olivia, I had every reason to expect Miss Richland's refusal, as I did everything in my power to deserve it. Her indelicacy surprises me!

OLIVIA. Sure, Leontine, there's nothing so indelicate in being sensible of your merit. If so, I fear, I shall be the most guilty thing alive!

LEONT. But you mistake, my dear. The same attention I used to advance my merit with you, I practised to lessen it with her. What more could I do?

OLIVIA. Let us now rather consider what's to be done. We have both dissembled too long—I have always been asham'd—I am now quite weary of it. Sure, I could never have undergone so much for any other but you.

LEONT. And you shall find my gratitude equal to your kindest compliance. Though our friends should totally forsake us, Olivia, we can draw upon content for the deficiencies of fortune.

OLIVIA. Then why should we defer our scheme of humble happiness, when it is now in our power? I may be the favourite of your father, it is true; but can it ever be thought, that his present kindness to a supposed child, will continue to a known deceiver?

LEONT. I have many reasons to believe it will. As his attachments are but few, they are lasting. His own marriage was a private one, as ours may be. Besides, I have sounded him already at a distance, and find all his answers exactly to our wish. Nay, by an expression or two that dropped from him, I am induced to think he knows of this affair.

OLIVIA. Indeed! But that would be an happiness too great to be expected.

LEONT. However it be, I'm certain you have power over him; and am persuaded, if you informed him of our situation, that he would be disposed to pardon it.

OLIVIA. You had equal expectations, Leontine, from your last scheme with Miss Richland, which you find has succeeded most wretchedly.

LEONT. And that's the best reason for trying another.

OLIVIA. If it must be so, I submit.

LEONT. As we could wish, he comes this way. Now, my dearest Olivia, be resolute. I'll just retire within hearing, to come in at a proper time, either to share your danger, or confirm your victory.   [*Exit.*

Enter CROAKER.

CROAKER. Yes, I must forgive her; and yet not too easily, neither. It will be proper to keep up the decorums of resentment a little, if it be only to impress her with an idea of my authority.

OLIVIA. How I tremble to approach him!—Might I presume, sir—if I interrupt you—

CROAKER. No, child, where I have an affection, it is not

a little thing can interrupt me. Affection gets over little things.

OLIVIA. Sir, you're too kind! I'm sensible how ill I deserve this partiality. Yet, Heaven knows, there is nothing I would not do to gain it.

CROAKER. And you have but too well succeeded, you little hussy, you! With those endearing ways of yours, on my conscience, I could be brought to forgive anything, unless it were a very great offence indeed.

OLIVIA. But mine is such an offence—when you know my guilt—yes, you shall know it, though I feel the greatest pain in the confession.

CROAKER. Why, then, if it be so very great a pain, you may spare yourself the trouble, for I know every syllable of the matter before you begin.

OLIVIA. Indeed! Then I'm undone!

CROAKER. Ay, miss, you wanted to steal a match, without letting me know it, did you! But I'm not worth being consulted, I suppose, when there's to be a marriage in my own family! No, I'm to have no hand in the disposal of my own children! No, I'm nobody! I'm to be a mere article of family lumber; a piece of cracked china to be stuck up in a corner!

OLIVIA. Dear sir, nothing but the dread of your authority could induce us to conceal it from you.

CROAKER. No, no, my consequence is no more; I'm as little minded as a dead Russian in winter, just stuck up with a pipe in his mouth till there comes a thaw—it goes to my heart to vex her.

OLIVIA. I was prepared, sir, for your anger, and despaired of pardon, even while I presumed to ask it. But your severity shall never abate my affection, as my punishment is but justice.

CROAKER. And yet you should not despair neither, Livy. We ought to hope all for the best.

OLIVIA. And do you permit me to hope, sir! Can I ever expect to be forgiven? But hope has too long deceived me!

CROAKER. Why then, child, I shan't deceive you now, for I forgive you this very moment. I forgive you all; and now you are indeed my daughter.

OLIVIA. O transport! This kindness overpowers me!

CROAKER. I was always against severity to our children. We have been young and giddy ourselves, and we can't expect boys and girls to be old before their time.

OLIVIA. What generosity! But can you forget the many falsehoods, the dissimulation——

CROAKER. You did indeed dissemble, you urchin, you; but where's the girl that won't dissemble for a husband! My wife and I had never been married, if we had not dissembled a little beforehand!

OLIVIA. It shall be my future care never to put such generosity to a second trial. And as for the partner of my offence and folly, from his native honour, and the just sense he has of his duty, I can answer for him that——

Enter LEONTINE.

LEONT. Permit him thus to answer for himself. (*Kneeling.*) Thus, sir, let me speak my gratitude for this unmerited forgiveness. Yes, sir, this even exceeds all your former tenderness: I now can boast the most indulgent of fathers. The life, he gave, compared to this, was but a trifling blessing!

CROAKER. And, good sir, who sent for you, with that fine tragedy face, and flourishing manner? I don't know what we have to do with your gratitude upon this occasion!

LEONT. How, sir! is it possible to be silent when so much

obliged? Would you refuse me the pleasure of being grateful? Of adding my thanks to my Olivia's! Of sharing in the transports that you have thus occasioned?

CROAKER. Lord, sir, we can be happy enough, without your coming in to make up the party. I don't know what's the matter with the boy all this day; he has got into such a rhodomontade manner all the morning!

LEONT. But, sir, I that have so large a part in the benefit, is it not my duty to show my joy? Is the being admitted to your favour so slight an obligation? Is the happiness of marrying my Olivia so small a blessing?

CROAKER. Marrying Olivia! marrying Olivia! marrying his own sister! Sure the boy is out of his senses. His own sister!

LEONT. My sister!

OLIVIA. Sister! How have I been mistaken! (*Aside.*)

LEONT. Some cursed mistake in this I find. (*Aside.*)

CROAKER. What does the booby mean, or has he any meaning. Eh, what do you mean, you blockhead, you?

LEONT. Mean, sir—why, sir—only when my sister is to be married, that I have the pleasure of marrying her, sir; that is, of giving her away, sir—I have made a point of it.

CROAKER. O, is that all? Give her away. You have made a point of it. Then you had as good make a point of first giving away yourself, as I'm going to prepare the writings between you and Miss Richland this very minute. What a fuss is here about nothing! Why, what's the matter now? I thought I had made you at least as happy as you could wish.

OLIVIA. O! yes, sir, very happy.

CROAKER. Do you foresee anything, child? You look as if you did. I think if anything was to be foreseen, I have as sharp a look out as another: and yet I foresee nothing.

[*Exit.*

LEONTINE, OLIVIA.

OLIVIA. What can it mean?

LEONT. He knows something, and yet for my life, I can't tell what.

OLIVIA. It can't be the connection between us, I'm pretty certain.

LEONT. Whatever it be, my dearest, I'm resolved to put it out of fortune's power to repeat our mortification. I'll haste, and prepare for our journey to Scotland this very evening. My friend Honeywood has promised me his advice and assistance. I'll go to him, and repose our distresses on his friendly bosom: and I know so much of his honest heart, that if he can't relieve our uneasinesses, he will at least share them.   [*Exeunt.*

END OF THE SECOND ACT

ACT THE THIRD

BAILIFF, HONEYWOOD, FOLLOWER.

BAILIFF. Looky, sir, I have arrested as good men as you in my time: no disparagement of you neither. Men that would go forty guineas on a game of cribbage. I challenge the town to shew a man in more genteeler practice than myself!

HONEYW. Without all question, Mr——I forget your name, sir?

BAILIFF. How can you forget what you never knew? he, he, he!

HONEYW. May I beg leave to ask your name?

BAILIFF. Yes, you may.

HONEYW. Then, pray, sir, what is your name, sir?

BAILIFF. That I didn't promise to tell you. He, he, he! A joke breaks no bones, as we say among us that practice the law.

HONEYW. You may have reason for keeping it a secret, perhaps?

BAILIFF. The law does nothing without reason. I'm ashamed to tell my name to no man, sir. If you can shew cause, as why, upon a special capus, that I should prove my name—But, come, Timothy Twitch is my name. And, now you know my name, what have you to say to that?

HONEYW. Nothing in the world, good Mr Twitch, but that I have a favour to ask, that's all.

BAILIFF. Ay, favours are more easily asked than granted,

as we say among us that practice the law. I have taken an oath against granting favours. Would you have me perjure myself?

Honeyw. But my request will come recommended in so strong a manner, as I believe you'll have no scruple (*pulling out his purse*). The thing is only this: I believe I shall be able to discharge this trifle in two or three days at farthest; but as I would not have the affair known for the world, I have thoughts of keeping you, and your good friend here, about me, till the debt is discharged; for which I shall be properly grateful.

Bailiff. Oh! that's another maxum, and altogether within my oath. For certain, if an honest man is to get anything by a thing, there's no reason why all things should not be done in civility.

Honeyw. Doubtless, all trades must live, Mr Twitch; and yours is a necessary one.　　　　　　[*Gives him money.*

Bailiff. Oh! your honour; I hope your honour takes nothing amiss as I does, as I does nothing but my duty in so doing. I'm sure no man can say I ever give a gentleman, that was a gentleman, ill usage. If I saw that a gentleman was a gentleman, I have taken money not to see him for ten weeks together.

Honeyw. Tenderness is a virtue, Mr Twitch.

Bailiff. Ay, sir, it's a perfect treasure. I love to see a gentleman with a tender heart. I don't know, but I think I have a tender heart myself. If all that I have lost by my heart was put together, it would make a—but no matter for that.

Honeyw. Don't account it lost, Mr Twitch. The ingratitude of the world can never deprive us of the conscious happiness of having acted with humanity ourselves.

Bailiff. Humanity, sir, is a jewel. It's better than gold. I love humanity. People may say that we in our way have no humanity; but I'll show you my humanity this moment. There's my follower here, little Flanigan, with a wife and four children, a guinea or two would be more to him, than twice as much to another. Now, as I can't shew him any humanity myself, I must beg leave you'll do it for me.

HONEYW. I assure you, Mr Twitch, yours is a most powerful recommendation.   [*Giving money to the follower.*

BAILIFF. Sir, you're a gentleman. I see you know what to do with your money. But, to business: we are to be with you here as your friends, I suppose. But set in case company comes.—Little Flanigan here, to be sure, has a good face, a very good face: but then, he is a little seedy, as we say among us that practice the law. Not well in clothes. Smoke the pocket holes.

HONEYW. Well, that shall be remedied without delay.

Enter SERVANT.

SERVANT. Sir, Miss Richland is below.

HONEYW. How unlucky! Detain her a moment. We must improve, my good friend, little Mr Flanigan's appearance first. Here, let Mr Flanigan have a suit of my clothes —quick—the brown and silver—Do you hear?

SERVANT. That your honour gave away to the begging gentleman that makes verses, because it was as good as new.

HONEYW. The white and gold, then.

SERVANT. That, your honour, I made bold to sell, because it was good for nothing.

HONEYW. Well, the first that comes to hand, then. The blue and gold. I believe Mr Flanigan will look best in blue.
      [*Exit* FLANIGAN.

BAILIFF. Rabbit me, but little Flanigan will look well in anything. Ah, if your honour knew that bit of flesh as well as I do, you'd be perfectly in love with him. There's not a prettier scout in the four counties after a shy-cock than he. Scents like a hound; sticks like a weazel. He was master of the ceremonies to the black queen of Morocco when I took him to follow me. (*Re-enter* FLANIGAN.) Heh, ecod, I think he looks so well, that I don't care if I have a suit from the same place for myself.

HONEYW. Well, well, I hear the lady coming. Dear Mr Twitch, I beg you'll give your friend directions not to speak. As for yourself, I know you will say nothing without being directed.

BAILIFF. Never you fear me, I'll shew the lady that I have something to say for myself as well as another. One man has one way of talking, and another man has another, that's all the difference between them.

Enter MISS RICHLAND *and her* MAID.

MISS RICH. You'll be surprised, sir, with this visit. But you know I'm yet to thank you for choosing my little library.

HONEYW. Thanks, madam, are unnecessary, as it was I that was obliged by your commands. Chairs here. Two of my very good friends, Mr Twitch and Mr Flanigan. Pray, gentlemen, sit without ceremony.

MISS RICH. (*aside*). Who can these odd-looking men be? I fear it is as I was informed. It must be so.

BAILIFF (*after a pause*). Pretty weather, very pretty weather for the time of the year, madam.

FOLLOWER. Very good circuit weather in the country.

HONEYW. You officers are generally favourites among the ladies. My friends, madam, have been upon very disagreeable duty, I assure you. The fair should, in some measure, recompense the toils of the brave.

MISS RICH. Our officers do indeed deserve every favour. The gentlemen are in the marine service, I presume, sir?

HONEYW. Why, madam, they do—occasionally serve in the Fleet, madam! A dangerous service!

MISS RICH. I'm told so. And I own, it has often surprised me, that, while we have had so many instances of bravery there, we have had so few of wit at home to praise it.

HONEYW. I grant, madam, that our poets have not written as our soldiers have fought; but they have done all they could, and Hawke or Amherst could do no more.

MISS RICH. I'm quite displeased when I see a fine subject spoiled by a dull writer.

HONEYW. We should not be so severe against dull writers, madam. It is ten to one, but the dullest writer exceeds the most rigid French critic who presumes to despise him.

FOLLOWER. Damn the French, the parle-vous, and all that belongs to them!

MISS RICH. Sir!

HONEYW. Ha, ha, ha, honest Mr Flanigan! A true English officer, madam; he's not contented with beating the French, but he will scold them too.

MISS RICH. Yet, Mr Honeywood, this does not convince me but that severity in criticism is necessary. It was our first adopting the severity of French taste, that has brought them in turn to taste us.

BAILIFF. Taste us! By the Lord, madam, they devour us! Give Monseers but a taste, and I'll be damned, but they come in for a bellyful!

MISS RICH. Very extraordinary, this!

FOLLOWER. But very true. What makes the bread rising: the parle-vous that devour us. What makes the mutton fivepence a pound: the parle-vous that eat it up. What makes the beer three pence half-penny a pot——

HONEYW. Ah! the vulgar rogues, all will be out! Right,

gentlemen, very right, upon my word, and quite to the purpose. They draw a parallel, madam, between the mental taste, and that of our senses. We are injured as much by French severity in the one, as by French rapacity in the other. That's their meaning.

Miss Rich. Though I don't see the force of the parallel, yet, I'll own, that we should sometimes pardon books, as we do our friends, that have now and then agreeable absurdities to recommend them.

Bailiff. That's all my eye! The King only can pardon, as the law says; for set in case——

Honeyw. I'm quite of your opinion, sir! I see the whole drift of your argument. Yes, certainly, our presuming to pardon any work, is arrogating a power that belongs to another. If all have power to condemn, what writer can be free?

Bailiff. By his habus corpus. His habus corpus can set him free at any time. For set in case——

Honeyw. I'm obliged to you, sir, for the hint. If, madam, as my friend observes, our laws are so careful of a gentleman's person, sure we ought to be equally careful of his dearer part, his fame.

Follower. Ay, but if so be a man's nabbed, you know——

Honeyw. Mr Flanigan, if you spoke for ever, you could not improve the last observation. For my own part, I think it conclusive.

Bailiff. As for the matter of that, mayhap——

Honeyw. Nay, sir, give me leave in this instance to be positive. For where is the necessity of censuring works without genius, which must shortly sink of themselves: what is it, but aiming our unnecessary blow against a victim already under the hands of justice?

Bailiff. Justice! O, by the elevens, if you talk about justice, I think I am at home there; for, in a course of law——

HONEYW. My dear Mr Twitch, I discern what you'd be at perfectly, and I believe the lady must be sensible of the art with which it is introduced. I suppose you perceive the meaning, madam, of his course of law?

MISS RICH. I protest, sir, I do not. I perceive only that you answer one gentleman before he has finished, and the other before he has well begun!

BAILIFF. Madam, you are a gentlewoman, and I will make the matter out. This here question is about severity and justice, and pardon, and the like of they. Now, to explain the thing——

HONEYW. (*aside*). O! curse your explanations.

Enter SERVANT.

SERVANT. Mr Leontine, sir, below, desires to speak with you upon earnest business.

HONEYW. That's lucky. (*Aside.*)—Dear madam, you'll excuse me, and my good friends here, for a few minutes. There are books, madam, to amuse you. Come, gentlemen, you know I make no ceremony with such friends. After you, sir. Excuse me. Well, if I must. But I know your natural politeness!

BAILIFF. Before and behind, you know.

FOLLOWER. Ay, ay, before and behind, before and behind!

[*Exeunt* HONEYWOOD, BAILIFF, *and* FOLLOWER.

MISS RICH. What can all this mean, Garnet?

GAR. Mean, madam? why, what should it mean, but what Mr Lofty sent you here to see? These people he calls officers, are officers sure enough: sheriff's officers; bailiffs, madam!

MISS RICH. Ay, it is certainly so. Well, though his perplexities are far from giving me pleasure, yet, I own, there's something very ridiculous in them, and a just punishment for his dissimulation.

GAR. And so they are. But I wonder, madam, that the lawyer you just employed to pay his debts, and set him free, has not done it by this time. He ought at least to have been here before now. But lawyers are always more ready to get a man into troubles, than out of them!

Enter SIR WILLIAM.

SIR WILL. For Miss Richland to undertake setting him free, I own, was quite unexpected. It has totally unhinged my schemes to reclaim him. Yet, it gives me pleasure to find, that, among a number of worthless friendships, he has made one acquisition of real value; for there must be some softer passion on her side that prompts this generosity. Ha! here before me: I'll endeavour to sound her affections. Madam, as I am the person that have had some demands upon the gentleman of this house, I hope you'll excuse me, if, before I enlarged him, I wanted to see yourself!

MISS RICH. The precaution was very unnecessary, sir! I suppose your wants were only such as my agent had power to satisfy.

SIR WILL. Partly, madam. But I was also willing you should be fully apprized of the character of the gentleman you intended to serve.

MISS RICH. It must come, sir, with a very ill grace from you. To censure it, after what you have done, would look like malice; and to speak favourably of a character you have oppressed, would be impeaching your own. And, sure, his tenderness, his humanity, his universal friendship, may atone for many faults!

SIR WILL. That friendship, madam, which is exerted in too wide a sphere, becomes totally useless. Our bounty, like a drop of water, disappears when diffused too widely. They, who pretend most to this universal benevolence, are either deceivers, or dupes. Men who desire to cover their private ill-nature, by a pretended regard for all; or, men who, reasoning themselves into false feelings, are more earnest in pursuit of splendid, than of useful virtues.

Miss Rich. I am surprised, sir, to hear one who has probably been a gainer by the folly of others, so severe in his censure of it.

Sir Will. Whatever I may have gained by folly, madam, you see I am willing to prevent your losing by it.

Miss Rich. Your cares for me, sir, are unnecessary! I always suspect those services which are denied where they are wanted, and offered, perhaps in hopes of a refusal. No, sir, my directions have been given, and I insist upon their being complied with.

Sir Will. Thou amiable woman! I can no longer contain the expressions of my gratitude: my pleasure. You see before you, one who has been equally careful of his interest: one who has for some time been a concealed spectator of his follies, and only punished in hopes to reclaim them— His uncle!

Miss Rich. Sir William Honeywood! You amaze me. How shall I conceal my confusion? I fear, sir, you'll think I have been too forward in my services, I confess I——

Sir Will. Don't make any apologies, madam. I only find myself unable to repay the obligation. And yet, I have been trying my interest of late to serve you. Having learnt, madam, that you had some demands upon government, I have, though unasked, been your solicitor there.

Miss Rich. Sir, I'm infinitely obliged to your intentions. But my guardian has employed another gentleman who assures him of success.

Sir Will. Who, the important little man that visits here! Trust me, madam, he's quite contemptible among men in power, and utterly unable to serve you. Mr Lofty's promises are much better known to people of fashion than his person, I assure you.

Miss Rich. How have we been deceived! As sure as can be, here he comes.

Sir Will. Does he? Remember I'm to continue unknown. My return to England has not as yet been made public. With what impudence he enters!

Enter Lofty.

Lofty. Let the chariot—let my chariot drive off, I'll visit to his Grace's in a chair. Miss Richland here before me! Punctual, as usual, to the calls of humanity. I'm very sorry, madam, things of this kind should happen, especially to a man I have shewn everywhere, and carried amongst us as a particular acquaintance.

Miss Rich. I find, sir, you have the art of making the misfortunes of others your own.

Lofty. My dear madam, what can a private man like me, do? One man can't do everything; and then, I do so much in this way every day: Let me see, something considerable might be done for him by subscription; it could not fail if I carried the list. I'll undertake to set down a brace of dukes, two dozen lords, and half the lower house, at my own peril!

Sir Will. And after all, it's more than probable, sir, he might reject the offer of such powerful patronage.

Lofty. Then, madam, what can we do? You know I never make promises. In truth, I once or twice tried to do something with him in the way of business; but, as I often told his uncle, Sir William Honeywood, the man was utterly impracticable.

SIR WILL. His uncle! Then that gentleman, I suppose, is a particular friend of yours.

LOFTY. Meaning me, sir?—Yes, madam, as I often said, my dear Sir William, you are sensible I would do anything as far as my poor interest goes, to serve your family; but what can be done? there's no procuring first-rate places for ninth-rate abilities.

MISS RICH. I have heard of Sir William Honeywood; he's abroad in employment; he confided in your judgment, I suppose.

LOFTY. Why, yes, madam; I believe Sir William has some reason to confide in my judgment; one little reason, perhaps.

MISS RICH. Pray, sir, what was it?

LOFTY. Why, madam—but let it go no further—it was I procured him his place.

SIR WILL. Did you, sir?

LOFTY. Either you or I, sir.

MISS RICH. This, Mr Lofty, was very kind, indeed.

LOFTY. I did love him, to be sure; he had some amusing qualities; no man was fitter to be toast-master to a club, or had a better head.

MISS RICH. A better head?

LOFTY. Ay, at a bottle. To be sure, he was as dull as a choice spirit; but hang it, he was grateful, very grateful; and gratitude hides a multitude of faults!

SIR WILL. He might have reason, perhaps. His place is pretty considerable, I'm told.

LOFTY. A trifle, a mere trifle, among us men of business. The truth is, he wanted dignity to fill up a greater.

SIR WILL. Dignity of person, do you mean, sir? I'm told he's much about my size and figure, sir.

LOFTY. Ay, tall enough for a marching regiment; but

then he wanted a something—a consequence of form—a kind of a—I believe the lady perceives my meaning.

Miss Rich. O perfectly! you courtiers can do anything, I see!

Lofty. My dear madam, all this is but a mere exchange; we do greater things for one another every day. Why, as thus, now: let me suppose you the first lord of the Treasury, you have an employment in you that I want; I have a place in me that you want; do me here, do you there: interest of both sides, few words, flat, done and done, and its over.

Sir Will. A thought strikes me. (*Aside.*)—Now you mention Sir William Honeywood, madam; and as he seems, sir, an acquaintance of yours; you'll be glad to hear he's arrived from Italy; I had it from a friend who knows him as well as he does me, and you may depend on my information.

Lofty. The devil he is!—If I had known that, we should not have been quite so well acquainted. (*Aside.*)

Sir Will. He is certainly returned; and as this gentleman is a friend of yours, he can be of signal service to us, by introducing me to him; there are some papers relative to your affairs, that require dispatch and his inspection.

Miss Rich. This gentleman, Mr Lofty, is a person employed in my affairs: I know you'll serve us!

Lofty. My dear madam, I live but to serve you. Sir William shall even wait upon him, if you think proper to command it.

Sir Will. That would be quite unnecessary.

Lofty. Well, we must introduce you, then. Call upon me—let me see—ay, in two days.

Sir Will. Now, or the opportunity will be lost for ever.

Lofty. Well, if it must be now, now let it be. But, damn it, that's unfortunate; my lord Grig's cursed Pensacola business comes on this very hour, and I'm engaged to attend
—another time—

SIR WILL. A short letter to Sir William will do.

LOFTY. You shall have it; yet, in my opinion, a letter is a very bad way of going to work; face to face, that's my way.

SIR WILL. The letter, sir, will do quite as well.

LOFTY. Zounds, sir, do you pretend to direct me; direct me in the business of office? Do you know me, sir? who am I?

MISS RICH. Dear Mr Lofty, this request is not so much his as mine; if my commands—but you despise my power.

LOFTY. Delicate creature! your commands could even control a debate at midnight; to a power so constitutional, I am all obedience and tranquillity. He shall have a letter; where is my secretary? Dubardieu! And yet I protest I don't like this way of doing business. I think if I spoke first to Sir William—But you will have it so.

[*Exit with* MISS RICH.

SIR WILLIAM *alone.*

SIR WILL. Ha, ha, ha! This, too, is one of my nephew's hopeful associates. O vanity, thou constant deceiver, how do all thy efforts to exalt, serve but to sink us. Thy false colourings, like those employed to heighten beauty, only seem to mend that bloom which they contribute to destroy. I'm not displeased at this interview; exposing this fellow's impudence to the contempt it deserves, may be of use to my design; at least, if he can reflect, it will be of use to himself.

Enter JARVIS.

SIR WILL. How now, Jarvis, where's your master, my nephew?

JARVIS. At his wit's end, I believe; he's scarce gotten ou of one scrape, but he's running his head into another.

SIR WILL. How so?

JARVIS. The house has but just been cleared of the bailiffs, and now he's again engaging tooth and nail in assisting old Croaker's son to patch up a clandestine match with the young lady that passes in the house for his sister!

Sir Will. Ever busy to serve others.

Jarvis. Ay, anybody but himself. The young couple, it seems, are just setting out for Scotland, and he supplies them with money for the journey.

Sir Will. Money! how is he able to supply others, who has scarce any for himself?

Jarvis. Why, there it is; he has no money, that's true; but then, as he never said no to any request in his life, he has given them a bill drawn by a friend of his upon a merchant in the city, which I am to get changed; for you must know that I am to go with them to Scotland myself.

Sir Will. How!

Jarvis. It seems the young gentleman is obliged to take a different road from his mistress, as he is to call upon an uncle of his that lives out of the way, in order to prepare a place for their reception, when they return; so they have borrowed me from my master, as the properest person to attend the young lady down.

Sir Will. To the land of matrimony! A pleasant journey, Jarvis.

Jarvis. Ay, but I'm only to have all the fatigues on't.

Sir Will. Well, it may be shorter, and less fatiguing than you imagine. I know but too much of the young lady's family and connexions, whom I have seen abroad. I have also discovered that Miss Richland is not indifferent to my thoughtless nephew: and will endeavour, though I fear, in vain, to establish that connexion. But, come, the letter I wait for must be almost finished; I'll let you further into my intentions, in the next room.   [*Exeunt.*

END OF THE THIRD ACT

ACT THE FOURTH

SCENE: CROAKER'S HOUSE

LOFTY.

LOFTY. Well, sure the devil's in me of late, for running my head into such defiles, as nothing but a genius like my own could draw me from. I was formerly contented to husband out my places and pensions with some degree of frugality; but, curse it, of late I have given away the whole Court Register in less time than they could print the title page; yet, hang it, why scruple a lie or two to come at a fine girl, when I every day tell a thousand for nothing. Ha! Honeywood here before me. Could Miss Richland have set him at liberty?

Enter HONEYWOOD.

Mr Honeywood, I'm glad to see you abroad again. I find my concurrence was not necessary in your unfortunate affairs. I had put things in a train to do your business; but it is not for me to say what I intended doing.

HONEYW. It was unfortunate, indeed, sir. But what adds to my uneasiness is, that while you seem to be acquainted with my misfortune, I, myself, continue still a stranger to my benefactor.

LOFTY. How! not know the friend that served you?

HONEYW. Can't guess at the person.

LOFTY. Enquire.

HONEYW. I have, but all I can learn is, that he chooses to remain concealed, and that all enquiry must be fruitless.

LOFTY. Must be fruitless?

Honeyw. Absolutely fruitless.

Lofty. Sure of that?

Honeyw. Very sure.

Lofty. Then I'll be damned if you shall ever know it from me.

Honeyw. How, sir!

Lofty. I suppose, now, Mr Honeywood, you think my rent-roll very considerable, and that I have vast sums of money to throw away; I know you do. The world, to be sure, says such things of me.

Honeyw. The world, by what I learn, is no stranger to your generosity. But where does this tend?

Lofty. To nothing; nothing in the world. The town, to be sure, when it makes such a thing as me the subject of conversation, has asserted, that I never yet patronized a man of merit.

Honeyw. I have heard instances to the contrary, even from yourself.

Lofty. Yes, Honeywood, and there are instances to the contrary that you shall never hear from myself.

Honeyw. Ha, dear sir, permit me to ask you but one question.

Lofty. Sir, ask me no questions: I say, sir, ask me no questions; I'll be damned if I answer them!

Honeyw. I will ask no further. My friend, my benefactor, it is, it must be here, that I am indebted for freedom, for honour. Yes, thou worthiest of men, from the beginning I suspected it, but was afraid to return thanks; which, if undeserved, might seem reproaches.

Lofty. I protest I don't understand all this, Mr Honeywood! You treat me very cavalierly. I do assure you, sir.— Blood, sir, can't a man be permitted to enjoy the luxury of his own feelings without all this parade?

HONEYW. Nay, do not attempt to conceal an action that adds to your honour. Your looks, your air, your manner, all confess it.

LOFTY. Confess it, sir! Torture itself, sir, shall never bring me to confess it. Mr Honeywood, I have admitted you upon terms of friendship. Don't let us fall out; make me happy, and let this be buried in oblivion. You know I hate ostentation; you know I do. Come, come, Honeywood, you know I always loved to be a friend, and not a patron. I beg this may make no kind of distance between us. Come, come, you and I must be more familiar—Indeed we must.

HONEYW. Heavens! Can I ever repay such friendship! Is there any way! Thou best of men, can I ever return the obligation?

LOFTY. A bagatelle, a mere bagatelle. But I see your heart is labouring to be grateful. You shall be grateful. It would be cruel to disappoint you.

HONEYW. How! Teach me the manner. Is there any way?

LOFTY. From this moment you're mine. Yes, my friend, you shall know it—I'm in love!

HONEYW. And can I assist you?

LOFTY. Nobody so well.

HONEYW. In what manner? I'm all impatience.

LOFTY. You shall make love for me.

HONEYW. And to whom shall I speak in your favour?

LOFTY. To a lady with whom you have great interest, I assure you. Miss Richland!

HONEYW. Miss Richland!

LOFTY. Yes, Miss Richland. She has struck the blow up to the hilt in my bosom, by Jupiter!

HONEYW. Heavens! was ever anything more unfortunate! It is too much to be endured.

LOFTY. Unfortunate, indeed! And yet I can endure it, till

you have opened the affair to her for me. Between ourselves, I think she likes me. I'm not apt to boast, but I think she does.

HONEYW. Indeed! But do you know the person you apply to?

LOFTY. Yes, I know you are her friend and mine: that's enough. To you, therefore, I commit the success of my passion. I'll say no more, let friendship do the rest. I have only to add, that if at any time my little interest can be of service—but, hang it, I'll make no promises—you know my interest is yours at any time. No apologies, my friend, I'll not be answered, it shall be so.   [*Exit.*

HONEYW. Open, generous, unsuspecting man! He little thinks that I love her too; and with such an ardent passion! —But then it was ever but a vain and hopeless one; my torment, my persecution! What shall I do! Love, friendship, a hopeless passion, a deserving friend! Love, that has been my tormentor; a friend, that has, perhaps, distressed himself to serve me. It shall be so. Yes, I will discard the fondling hope from my bosom, and exert all my influence in his favour. And yet to see her in the possession of another!— Insupportable. But then to betray a generous, trusting friend!—Worse, worse. Yes, I'm resolved. Let me but be the instrument of their happiness, and then quit a country, where I must for ever despair of finding my own.   [*Exit.*

Enter OLIVIA *and* GARNET, *who carries a Milliner's Box.*

OLIVIA. Dear me, I wish this journey were over. No news of Jarvis yet? I believe the old peevish creature delays purely to vex me.

GAR. Why, to be sure, madam, I did hear him say a little snubbing before marriage would teach you to bear it the better afterwards.

OLIVIA. To be gone a full hour, though he had only to get a bill changed in the city! How provoking!

GAR. I'll lay my life, Mr Leontine, that had twice as much to do, is setting off by this time from his inn: and here you are left behind.

OLIVIA. Well, let us be prepared for his coming, however. Are you sure you have omitted nothing, Garnet?

GAR. Not a stick, madam—all's here. Yet I wish you could take the white and silver to be married in. It's the worst luck in the world, in anything but white. I knew one Bet Stubbs, of our town, that was married in red; and, as sure as eggs is eggs, the bridegroom and she had a miff before morning.

OLIVIA. No matter. I'm all impatience till we are out of the house.

GAR. Bless me, madam, I had almost forgot the wedding-ring!—The sweet little thing—I don't think it would go on my little finger. And what if I put in a gentleman's night-cap, in case of necessity, madam? But here's Jarvis.

Enter JARVIS.

OLIVIA. O, Jarvis, are you come at last? We have been ready this half hour. Now let's be going. Let us fly!

JARVIS. Aye, to Jericho! for we shall have no going to Scotland this bout, I fancy.

OLIVIA. How! What's the matter?

JARVIS. Money, money, is the matter, madam. We have got no money. What the plague do you send me of your fool's errand for? My master's bill upon the city is not worth a rush. Here it is; Mrs Garnet may pin up her hair with it.

OLIVIA. Undone! How could Honeywood serve us so! What shall we do? Can't we go without it?

JARVIS. Go to Scotland without money! To Scotland without money! Lord how some people understand geography! We might as well set sail for Patagonia upon a cork jacket.

OLIVIA. Such a disappointment! What a base insincere man was your master, to serve us in this manner. Is this his good nature?

JARVIS. Nay, don't talk ill of my master, madam. I won't bear to hear anybody talk ill of him but myself.

GAR. Bless us! now I think on't, madam, you need not be under any uneasiness: I saw Mr Leontine receive forty guineas from his father just before he set out, and he can't yet have left the inn. A short letter will reach him there.

OLIVIA. Well remembered, Garnet; I'll write immediately. How's this! Bless me, my hand trembles so, I can't write a word. Do you write, Garnet; and, upon second thought, it will be better from you.

GAR. Truly, madam, I write and indite but poorly. I never was kute in my larning. But I'll do what I can to please you. Let me see. All out of my own head, I suppose?

OLIVIA. Whatever you please.

GAR. (*writing*). Muster Croaker—Twenty guineas, madam?

OLIVIA. Ay, twenty will do.

GAR. At the bar of the Talbot till called for. Expedition —will be blown up—all of a flame—Quick, dispatch— Cupid, the little God of Love—I conclude it, madam, with Cupid; I love to see a love-letter end like poetry.

OLIVIA. Well, well, what you please, anything. But how shall we send it? I can trust none of the servants of this family.

GAR. Odso, madam, Mr Honeywood's butler is in the next room; he's a dear, sweet man; he'll do anything for me.

JARVIS. He! the dog, he'll certainly commit some blunder. He's drunk and sober ten times a day!

OLIVIA. No matter. Fly, Garnet; anybody we can trust will do. [*Exit* GARNET.] Well, Jarvis, now we can have nothing more to interrupt us. You may take up the things, and carry them on to the inn. Have you no hands, Jarvis?

JARVIS. Soft and fair, young lady. You, that are going to be married, think things can never be done too fast: but we that are old, and know what we are about, must elope methodically, madam.

OLIVIA. Well, sure, if my indiscretions were to be done over again——

JARVIS. My life for it you would do them ten times over.

OLIVIA. Why will you talk so? If you knew how unhappy they make me——

JARVIS. Very unhappy, no doubt: I was once just as unhappy when I was going to be married myself. I'll tell you a story about that——

OLIVIA. A story! when I'm all impatience to be away. Was there ever such a dilatory creature!——

JARVIS. Well, madam, if we must march, why we will march; that's all. Though, odds bobs we have still forgot one thing we should never travel without—a case of good razors, and a box of shaving-powder. But no matter, I believe we shall be pretty well shaved by the way.   [*Going.*

Enter GARNET.

GAR. Undone, undone, madam! Ah, Mr Jarvis, you said right enough. As sure as death Mr Honeywood's rogue of a drunken butler dropped the letter before he went ten yards from the door. There's old Croaker has just picked it up, and is this moment reading it to himself in the hall!

OLIVIA. Unfortunate! We shall be discovered!

GAR. No, madam; don't be uneasy, he can make neither head nor tail of it. To be sure he looks as if he was broke loose from Bedlam about it, but he can't find what it means for all that. O Lud, he is coming this way all in the horrors!

OLIVIA. Then let us leave the house this instant, for fear he should ask further questions. In the mean time, Garnet, do you write and send off just such another.   [*Exeunt.*

Enter CROAKER.

CROAKER. Death and destruction! Are all the horrors of air, fire and water to be levelled only at me! Am I only to be singled out for gunpowder-plots, combustibles, and conflagration! Here it is—An incendiary letter dropped at my door. *To Muster Croaker, these, with speed.* Ay, ay, plain enough the direction: all in the genuine incendiary spelling, and as cramp as the devil. *With speed.* O, confound your speed. But let me read it once more. (*Reads.*)

Mustar Croakar as sone as yoew see this leve twenty gunnes at the bar of the Talboot tell caled for or yowe and yower experetion will be al blown up! Ah, but too plain! Blood and gunpowder in every line of it. Blown up! murderous dog! All blown up! Heavens! what have I and my poor family done, to be all blown up? (*Reads.*) *Our pockets are low, and money we must have.* Ay, there's the reason; they'll blow us up, because they have got low pockets. (*Reads.*) *It is but a short time you have to consider; for if this takes wind, the house will quickly be all of a flame.* Inhuman monsters! blow us up, and then burn us. The earthquake at Lisbon was but a bonfire to it! (*Reads.*) *Make quick dispatch, and so no more at present. But may Cupid, the little God of Love, go with you wherever you go.* The little God of Love! Cupid, the little God of Love go with me! Go you to the devil, you and your little Cupid together; I'm so frightened, I scarce know whether I sit, stand, or go. Perhaps this moment I'm treading on lighted matches, blazing brimstone and barrels of gunpowder. They are preparing to blow me up into the clouds. Murder! We shall be all burnt in our beds; we shall be all burnt in our beds.

Enter MISS RICHLAND.

MISS RICH. Lord, sir, what's the matter?

CROAKER. Murder's the matter. We shall be all blown up in our beds before morning!

MISS RICH. I hope not, sir.

CROAKER. What signifies what you hope, madam, when I have a certificate of it here in my hand? Will nothing alarm my family? Sleeping and eating, sleeping and eating is the only work from morning till night in my house. My insensible crew could sleep, though rocked by an earthquake, and fry beef steaks at a volcano!

MISS RICH. But, sir, you have alarmed them so often already, we have nothing but earthquakes, famines, plagues, and mad dogs from year's end to year's end. You remember, sir, it is not above a month ago, that you assured us of a conspiracy among the bakers, to poison us in our bread; and so kept the whole family a week upon potatoes.

CROAKER. And potatoes were too good for them. But why do I stand talking here with a girl, when I should be facing the enemy without? Here, John, Nicodemus, search the house. Look into the cellars, to see if there be any combustibles below; and above, in the apartments, that no matches be thrown in at the windows. Let all the fires be put out, and let the engine be drawn out in the yard, to play upon the house in case of necessity.   [*Exit.*

Miss Richland *alone.*

Miss Rich. What can he mean by all this? Yet, why should I enquire, when he alarms us in this manner almost every day? But Honeywood has desired an interview with me in private. What can he mean; or, rather, what means this palpitation at his approach? It is the first time he ever shewed anything in his conduct that seemed particular. Sure he cannot mean to——but he's here.

Enter Honeywood.

Honeyw. I presumed to solicit this interview, madam, before I left town, to be permitted—
Miss Rich. Indeed! Leaving town, sir?—
Honeyw. Yes, madam; perhaps the kingdom. I have presumed, I say, to desire the favour of this interview—in order to disclose something which our long friendship prompts. And yet my fears—
Miss Rich. His fears! What are his fears to mine? (*Aside.*) —We have indeed been long acquainted, sir; very long. If I remember, our first meeting was at the French Ambassador's. —Do you recollect how you were pleased to rally me upon my complexion there?
Honeyw. Perfectly, madam; I presumed to reprove you for painting: but your warmer blushes soon convinced the company that the colouring was all from nature.
Miss Rich. And yet you only meant it, in your good-natur'd way, to make me pay a compliment to myself. In the same manner you danced that night with the most awkward woman in company, because you saw nobody else would take her out.
Honeyw. Yes; and was rewarded the next night, by

dancing with the finest woman in company, whom everybody wished to take out.

MISS RICH. Well, sir, if you thought so then, I fear your judgment has since corrected the errors of a first impression. We generally show to most advantage at first. Our sex are like poor tradesmen, that put all their best goods to be seen at the windows.

HONEYW. The first impression, madam, did indeed deceive me. I expected to find a woman with all the faults of conscious flattered beauty. I expected to find her vain and insolent. But every day has since taught me that it is possible to possess sense without pride, and beauty without affectation.

MISS RICH. This, sir, is a style unusual with Mr Honeywood; and I should be glad to know why he thus attempts to increase that vanity, which his own lessons have taught me to despise.

HONEYW. I ask pardon, madam. Yet, from our long friendship, I presumed I might have some right to offer, without offence, what you may refuse without offending.

MISS RICH. Sir! I beg you'd reflect; though, I fear, I shall scarce have any power to refuse a request of yours; yet, you may be precipitate: consider, sir.

HONEYW. I own my rashness; but, as I plead the cause of friendship, of one who loves—Don't be alarmed, madam —Who loves you with the most ardent passion; whose whole happiness is placed in you—

MISS RICH. I fear, sir, I shall never find whom you mean, by this description of him.

HONEYW. Ah, madam, it but too plainly points him out; though he should be too humble himself to urge his pretensions, or you too modest to understand them.

MISS RICH. Well; it would be affectation any longer to

pretend ignorance; and, I will own, sir, I have long been prejudiced in his favour. It was but natural to wish to make his heart mine, as he seemed himself ignorant of its value.

HONEYW. I see she always loved him! (*Aside*.)—I find, madam, you're already sensible of his worth, his passion. How happy is my friend, to be the favourite of one with such sense to distinguish merit, and such beauty to reward it!

MISS RICH. Your friend! sir. What friend?

HONEYW. My best friend—My friend Mr Lofty, madam.

MISS RICH. He, sir!

HONEYW. Yes, he, madam! He is, indeed, what your warmest wishes might have formed him. And to his other qualities, he adds that of the most passionate regard for you.

MISS RICH. Amazement!—No more of this, I beg you, sir.

HONEYW. I see your confusion, madam, and know how to interpret it. And since I so plainly read the language of your heart, shall I make my friend happy, by communicating your sentiments?

MISS RICH. By no means.

HONEYW. Excuse me; I must; I know you desire it.

MISS RICH. Mr Honeywood, let me tell you, that you wrong my sentiments and yourself. When I first applied to your friendship, I expected advice and assistance; but now, sir, I see that it is vain to expect happiness from him, who has been so bad an economist of his own; and that I must disclaim his friendship, who ceases to be a friend to himself.

[*Exit*.

HONEYW. How is this! she has confessed she loved him, and yet she seemed to part in displeasure. Can I have done anything to reproach myself with? No; I believe not; yet, after all, these things should not be done by a third person; I should have spared her confusion. My friendship carried me a little too far.

Enter CROAKER, *with the Letter in his Hand,*
and MRS CROAKER.

MRS CROAKER. Ha, ha, ha! And so, my dear, it's your supreme wish that I should be quite wretched upon this occasion? Ha, ha.

CROAKER (*mimicking*). Ha, ha, ha! and so, my dear, it's your supreme pleasure to give me no better consolation?

MRS CROAKER. Positively, my dear, what is this incendiary stuff and trumpery to me? Our house may travel through the air like the house of Loretto, for ought I care, if I'm to be miserable in it.

CROAKER. Would to Heaven it were converted into a house of correction for your benefit. Have we not everything to alarm us? Perhaps, this very moment, the tragedy is beginning.

MRS CROAKER. Then let us reserve our distress till the rising of the curtain, or give them the money they want, and have done with them.

CROAKER. Give them my money!—And pray, what right have they to my money?

MRS CROAKER. And pray, what right then have you to my good humour?

CROAKER. And so your good humour advises me to part with my money? Why, then, to tell your good humour a piece of my mind, I'd sooner part with my wife! Here's Mr Honeywood, see what he'll say to it. My dear Honeywood, look at this incendiary letter dropped at my door. It will freeze you with terror; and yet lovey here can read it—can read it, and laugh!

MRS CROAKER. Yes, and so will Mr Honeywood.

CROAKER. If he does, I'll suffer to be hanged the next minute in the rogue's place, that's all!

MRS CROAKER. Speak, Mr Honeywood! is there anything more foolish than my husband's fright upon this occasion?

HONEYW. It would not become me to decide, madam; but doubtless, the greatness of his terrors now, will but invite them to renew their villainy another time.

MRS CROAKER. I told you, he'd be of my opinion.

CROAKER. How, sir! do you maintain that I should lie down under such an injury, and shew, neither by my tears, or complaints, that I have something of the spirit of a man in me?

HONEYW. Pardon me, sir. You ought to make the loudest complaints, if you desire redress. The surest way to have redress, is to be earnest in the pursuit of it.

CROAKER. Ay, whose opinion is he of now?

MRS CROAKER. But don't you think that laughing off our fears is the best way?

HONEYW. What is the best, madam, few can say; but I'll maintain it to be a very wise way.

CROAKER. But we're talking of the best. Surely the best way is to face the enemy in the field, and not wait till he plunders us in our very bed chamber.

HONEYW. Why, sir, as to the best, that—that's a very wise way too.

MRS CROAKER. But can anything be more absurd, than to double our distresses by our apprehensions, and put it in the power of every low fellow, that can scrawl ten words of wretched spelling, to torment us?

HONEYW. Without doubt, nothing more absurd.

CROAKER. How! would it not be more absurd to despise the rattle till we are bit by the snake?

HONEYW. Without doubt, perfectly absurd.

CROAKER. Then you are of my opinion?

HONEYW. Entirely.

MRS CROAKER. And you reject mine?

HONEYW. Heaven forbid, madam. No, sure, no reasoning can be more just than yours. We ought certainly to despise malice if we cannot oppose it, and not make the incendiary's pen as fatal to our repose as the highwayman's pistol.

MRS CROAKER. O! then you think I'm quite right?

HONEYW. Perfectly right!

CROAKER. A plague of plagues, we can't be both right. I ought to be sorry, or I ought to be glad. My hat must be on my head, or my hat must be off.

MRS CROAKER. Certainly, in two opposite opinions, if one be perfectly reasonable, the other can't be perfectly right.

HONEYW. And why may not both be right, madam? Mr Croaker in earnestly seeking redress, and you in waiting the event with good humour? Pray let me see the letter again. I have it. This letter requires twenty guineas to be left at the bar of the Talbot inn. If it be indeed an incendiary letter, what if you and I, sir, go there; and, when the writer comes to be paid his expected booty, seize him?

CROAKER. My dear friend, it's the very thing; the very thing. While I walk by the door, you shall plant yourself in ambush near the bar; burst out upon the miscreant like a masked battery; extort a confession at once, and so hang him up by surprise.

HONEYW. Yes; but I would not choose to exercise too much severity. It is my maxim, sir, that crimes generally punish themselves.

CROAKER. Well, but we may upbraid him a little, I suppose? (*Ironically.*)

HONEYW. Ay, but not punish him too rigidly.

CROAKER. Well, well, leave that to my own benevolence.

Honeyw. Well, I do: but remember that universal benevolence is the first law of nature.

                [Exeunt Honeywood *and* Mrs Croaker.

Croaker. Yes; and my universal benevolence will hang the dog, if he had as many necks as a hydra!

END OF THE FOURTH ACT

ACT THE FIFTH

SCENE: AN INN

Enter OLIVIA, JARVIS.

OLIVIA. Well, we have got safe to the inn, however. Now, if the post-chaise were ready—

JARVIS. The horses are just finishing their oats; and, as they are not going to be married, they choose to take their own time.

OLIVIA. You are for ever giving wrong motives to my impatience.

JARVIS. Be as impatient as you will, the horses must take their own time; besides, you don't consider, we have got no answer from our fellow-traveller yet. If we hear nothing from Mr Leontine, we have only one way left us.

OLIVIA. What way?

JARVIS. The way home again.

OLIVIA. Not so. I have made a resolution to go, and nothing shall induce me to break it.

JARVIS. Ay; resolutions are well kept when they jump with inclination. However, I'll go hasten things without. And I'll call too at the bar to see if anything should be left for us there. Don't be in such a plaguy hurry, madam, and we shall go the faster, I promise you.   [*Exit* JARVIS.

Enter LANDLADY.

LANDLADY. What! Solomon; why don't you move? Pipes and tobacco for the Lamb there.— Will nobody answer? To the Dolphin; quick. The Angel has been outrageous this half hour. Did your ladyship call, madam?

Olivia. No, madam.

Landlady. I find, as you're for Scotland, madam—But, that's no business of mine; married, or not married, I ask no questions. To be sure, we had a sweet little couple set off from this two days ago for the same place. The gentleman, for a tailor, was, to be sure, as fine a spoken tailor, as ever blew froth from a full pot. And the young lady so bashful, it was near half an hour before we could get her to finish a pint of raspberry between us.

Olivia. But this gentleman and I are not going to be married, I assure you.

Landlady. May be not. That's no business of mine; for certain, Scotch marriages seldom turn out. There was, of my own knowledge, Miss Macfag, that married her father's footman.—Alack-a-day, she and her husband soon parted, and now keep separate cellars in Hedge Lane.

Olivia (*aside*). A very pretty picture of what lies before me.

Enter Leontine.

Leont. My dear Olivia, my anxiety till you were out of danger, was too great to be resisted. I could not help coming to see you set out, though it exposes us to a discovery.

Olivia. May everything you do prove as fortunate. Indeed, Leontine, we have been most cruelly disappointed. Mr Honeywood's bill upon the city, has, it seems, been protested, and we have been utterly at a loss how to proceed.

Leont. How! An offer of his own too. Sure, he could not mean to deceive us.

Olivia. Depend upon his sincerity; he only mistook the desire for the power of serving us. But let us think no more of it. I believe the post-chaise is ready by this.

Landlady. Not quite yet: and, begging your ladyship's

pardon, I don't think your ladyship quite ready for the post-chaise. The north road is a cold place, madam. I have a drop in the house of as pretty raspberry as ever was tipt over tongue. Just a thimbleful to keep the wind off your stomach. To be sure, the last couple we had here, they said it was a perfect nosegay. Ecod, I sent them both away as good-natur'd—Up went the blinds, round went the wheels, and drive away post-boy, was the word.

Enter CROAKER.

CROAKER. Well, while my friend Honeywood is upon the post of danger at the bar, it must be my business to have an eye about me here. I think I know an incendiary's look; for, wherever the devil makes a purchase, he never fails to set his mark. Ha! who have we here? My son and daughter! What can they be doing here?

LANDLADY. I tell you, madam, it will do you good; I think I know by this time what's good for the north road. It's a raw night, madam—sir—

LEONT. Not a drop more, good madam. I should now take it as a greater favour, if you hasten the horses, for I am afraid to be seen myself.

LANDLADY. That shall be done. Wha, Solomon! are you all dead there? Wha, Solomon, I say. [*Exit bawling*.

OLIVIA. Well; I dread lest an expedition begun in fear should end in repentance.—Every moment we stay increases our danger, and adds to my apprehensions.

LEONT. There's no danger, trust me, my dear; there can be none: if Honeywood has acted with honour, and kept my father, as he promised, in employment, till we are out of danger, nothing can interrupt our journey.

OLIVIA. I have no doubt of Mr Honeywood's sincerity, and even his desires to serve us. My fears are from your

5

father's suspicions. A mind so disposed to be alarmed without a cause, will be but too ready when there's a reason.

LEONT. Why, let him, when we are out of his power. But, believe me, Olivia, you have no great reason to dread his resentment. His repining temper, as it does no manner of injury to himself, so will it never do harm to others. He only frets to keep himself employed, and scolds for his private amusement.

OLIVIA. I don't know that; but, I'm sure, on some occasions, it makes him look most shockingly.

CROAKER (*discovering himself*). How does he look now?—How does he look now?

OLIVIA. Ah!

LEONT. Undone!

CROAKER. How do I look now? Sir, I am your very humble servant. Madam, I am yours. What, you are going off, are you? Then, first, if you please, take a word or two from me with you before you go. Tell me first where you are going, and when you have told me that, perhaps I shall know as little as I did before.

LEONT. If that be so, our answer might but increase your displeasure, without adding to your information.

CROAKER. I want no information from you, puppy; and you, too, good madam, what answer have you got? Eh! (*A cry without, stop him.*) I think I heard a noise. My friend, Honeywood, without—has he seized the incendiary? Ah, no, for now I hear no more on't.

LEONT. Honeywood, without! Then, sir, it was Mr Honeywood that directed you hither.

CROAKER. No, sir, it was Mr Honeywood conducted me hither.

LEONT. Is it possible?

CROAKER. Possible! Why, he's in the house now, sir. More anxious about me, than my own son, sir.

LEONT. Then, sir, he's a villain!

CROAKER. How, sirrah! a villain, because he takes most care of your father? I'll not bear it. I tell you I'll not bear it. Honeywood is a friend to the family, and I'll have him treated as such.

LEONT. I shall study to repay his friendship as it deserves.

CROAKER. Ah, rogue, if you knew how earnestly he entered into my griefs, and pointed out the means to detect them, you would love him as I do. (*A cry without, stop him.*) Fire and fury! they have seized the incendiary: they have the villain, the incendiary in view. Stop him, stop an incendiary, a murderer; stop him!   [*Exit.*

OLIVIA. Oh, my terrors! What can this new tumult mean?

LEONT. Some new mark, I suppose, of Mr Honeywood's sincerity. But we shall have satisfaction: he shall give me instant satisfaction.

OLIVIA. It must not be, my Leontine, if you value my esteem, or my happiness. Whatever be our fate, let us not add guilt to our misfortunes—Consider that our innocence will shortly be all we have left us. You must forgive him.

LEONT. Forgive him! Has he not in every instance betrayed us? Forced me to borrow money from him, which appears a mere trick to delay us: promised to keep my father engaged till we were out of danger, and here brought him to the very scene of our escape?

OLIVIA. Don't be precipitate. We may yet be mistaken

Enter POSTBOY, *dragging in* JARVIS: HONEYWOOD *entering soon after.*

POSTBOY. Ay, master, we have him fast enough. Here is the incendiary dog. I'm entitled to the reward; I'll take my oath I saw him ask for the money at the bar, and then run for it.

HONEYW. Come, bring him along. Let us see him. Let him learn to blush for his crimes. (*Discovering his mistake.*) Death! what's here! Jarvis, Leontine, Olivia! What can all this mean?

JARVIS. Why, I'll tell you what it means: that I was an old fool, and that you are my master—that's all.

HONEYW. Confusion!

LEONT. Yes, sir, I find you have kept your word with me. After such baseness, I wonder how you can venture to see the man you have injured.

HONEYW. My dear Leontine, by my life, my honour—

LEONT. Peace, peace, for shame; and do not continue to aggravate baseness by hypocrisy. I know you, sir, I know you.

HONEYW. Why, won't you hear me! By all that's just, I knew not—

LEONT. Hear you, sir! to what purpose? I now see through all your low arts; your ever complying with every opinion; your never refusing any request; your friendship as common as a prostitute's favours, and as fallacious; all these, sir, have long been contemptible to the world, and are now perfectly so to me.

HONEYW. (*aside*). Ha! contemptible to the world! That reaches me.

LEONT. All the seeming sincerity of your professions I now find were only allurements to betray; and all your seeming regret for their consequences, only calculated to cover the cowardice of your heart. Draw, villain!

Enter CROAKER *out of Breath.*

CROAKER. Where is the villain? Where is the incendiary? (*Seizing the postboy.*) Hold him fast, the dog; he has the gallows in his face. Come, you dog, confess; confess all, and hang yourself.

POSTBOY. Zounds! master, what do you throttle me for?

CROAKER (*beating him*). Dog, do you resist; do you resist?

POSTBOY. Zounds! master, I'm not he; there's the man that we thought was the rogue, and turns out to be one of the company.

CROAKER. How!

HONEYW. Mr Croaker, we have all been under a strange mistake here; I find there is nobody guilty; it was all an error; entirely an error of our own.

CROAKER. And I say, sir, that you're in an error: for there's guilt and double guilt, a plot, a damn'd Jesuitical pestilential plot, and I must have proof of it.

HONEYW. Do but hear me.

CROAKER. What, you intend to bring 'em off, I suppose; I'll hear nothing.

HONEYW. Madam, you seem at least calm enough to hear reason.

OLIVIA. Excuse me.

HONEYW. Good Jarvis, let me then explain it to you.

JARVIS. What signifies explanation, when the thing is done?

HONEYW. Will nobody hear me? Was there ever such a set, so blinded by passion and prejudice! (*To the postboy.*) My good friend, I believe you'll be surprised when I assure you—

POSTBOY. Sure me nothing—I'm sure of nothing but a good beating.

CROAKER. Come then, you, madam, if you ever hope for any favour or forgiveness, tell me sincerely all you know of this affair.

OLIVIA. Unhappily, sir, I'm but too much the cause of

your suspicions: you see before you, sir, one that with false pretences has stept into your family to betray it: not your daughter—

CROAKER. Not my daughter!

OLIVIA. Not your daughter—but a mean deceiver—who —support me, I cannot—

HONEYW. Help, she's going, give her air.

CROAKER. Ay, ay, take the young woman to the air; I would not hurt a hair of her head, whose ever daughter she may be—not so bad as that neither.

[*Exeunt all but* CROAKER.

CROAKER. Yes, yes, all's out; I now see the whole affair: my son is either married, or going to be so, to this lady, whom he imposed upon me as his sister. Ay, certainly so; and yet I don't find it afflicts me so much as one might think. There's the advantage of fretting away our misfortunes beforehand, we never feel them when they come.

Enter MISS RICHLAND *and* SIR WILLIAM.

SIR WILL. But how do you know, madam, that my nephew intends setting off from this place?

MISS RICH. My maid assured me he was come to this inn, and my own knowledge of his intending to leave the kingdom, suggested the rest. But what do I see, my guardian here before us! Who, my dear sir, could have expected meeting you here; to what accident do we owe this pleasure?

CROAKER. To a fool, I believe.

MISS RICH. But to what purpose did you come?

CROAKER. To play the fool.

MISS RICH. But with whom?

CROAKER. With greater fools than myself.

MISS RICH. Explain.

CROAKER. Why, Mr Honeywood brought me here, to do nothing now I am here; and my son is going to be married to I don't know who that is here; so now you are as wise as I am.

MISS RICH. Married! to whom, sir?

CROAKER. To Olivia; my daughter, as I took her to be; but who the devil she is, or whose daughter she is, I know no more than the man in the moon.

SIR WILL. Then, sir, I can inform you; and, though a stranger, yet you shall find me a friend to your family: it will be enough at present, to assure you, that, both in point of birth and fortune, the young lady is at least your son's equal. Being left by her father, Sir James Woodville—

CROAKER. Sir James Woodville! What, of the West?

SIR WILL. Being left by him, I say, to the care of a mercenary wretch, whose only aim was to secure her fortune to himself, she was sent into France, under pretence of education; and there every art was tried to fix her for life in a convent, contrary to her inclinations. Of this I was informed upon my arrival in Paris; and, as I had been once her father's friend, I did all in my power to frustrate her guardian's base intentions. I had even meditated to rescue her from his authority, when your son stept in with more pleasing violence, gave her liberty, and you a daughter.

CROAKER. But I intend to have a daughter of my own choosing, sir. A young lady, sir, whose fortune, by my interest with those that have interest, will be double what my son has a right to expect! Do you know Mr Lofty, sir?

SIR WILL. Yes, sir; and know that you are deceived in him. But step this way, and I'll convince you.

[CROAKER *and* SIR WILLIAM *seem to confer.*

Enter Honeywood.

Honeyw. Obstinate man, still to persist in his outrage! Insulted by him, despised by all, I now begin to grow contemptible, even to myself. How have I sunk by too great an assiduity to please! How have I overtaxed all my abilities, lest the approbation of a single fool should escape me! But all is now over; I have survived my reputation, my fortune, my friendships, and nothing remains henceforward for me but solitude and repentance.

Miss Rich. Is it true, Mr Honeywood, that you are setting off, without taking leave of your friends? The report is, that you are quitting England. Can it be?

Honeyw. Yes, madam; and though I am so unhappy as to have fallen under your displeasure, yet, thank Heaven, I leave you to happiness; to one who loves you, and deserves your love; to one who has power to procure you affluence, and generosity to improve your enjoyment of it.

Miss Rich. And you are sure, sir, that the gentleman you mean is what you describe him?

Honeyw. I have the best assurances of it, his serving me. He does indeed deserve the highest happiness, and that is in your power to confer. As for me, weak and wavering as I have been, obliged by all, and incapable of serving any, what happiness can I find but in solitude? What hope but in being forgotten?

Miss Rich. A thousand! to live among friends that esteem you, whose happiness it will be to be permitted to oblige you.

Honeyw. No, madam; my resolution is fixed. Inferiority among strangers is easy; but among those that once were equals, insupportable. Nay, to show you how far my resolution can go, I can now speak with calmness of my former follies, my vanity, my dissipation, my weakness. I will even confess, that, among the number of my other presumptions, I had the insolence to think of loving you. Yes, madam, while I was pleading the passion of another, my heart was tortured with its own. But it is over, it was unworthy our friendship, and let it be forgotten.

MISS RICH. You amaze me!

HONEYW. But you'll forgive it, I know you will; since the confession should not have come from me even now, but to convince you of the sincerity of my intention of—never mentioning it more.   [*Going.*

MISS RICH. Stay, sir, one moment—Ha! he here—

Enter LOFTY.

LOFTY. Is the coast clear? None but friends. I have followed you here with a trifling piece of intelligence: but it goes no farther, things are not yet ripe for a discovery. I have spirits working at a certain board; your affair at the Treasury will be done in less than—a thousand years. Mum!

MISS RICH. Sooner, sir, I should hope!

LOFTY. Why, yes, I believe it may, if it falls into proper hands, that know where to push and where to parry; that know how the land lies—eh, Honeywood?

MISS RICH. It is fallen into yours.

LOFTY. Well, to keep you no longer in suspense, your thing is done. It is done, I say—that's all. I have just had assurances from Lord Neverout, that the claim has been examined, and found admissible. *Quietus* is the word, madam.

HONEYW. But how! his lordship has been at Newmarket these ten days!

LOFTY. Indeed! Then Sir Gilbert Goose must have been most damnably mistaken. I had it of him.

MISS RICH. He! why Sir Gilbert and his family have been in the country this month!

LOFTY. This month! It must certainly be so—Sir Gilbert's letter did come to me from Newmarket, so that he must have met his lordship there; and so it came about. I have his letter about me, I'll read it to you. (*Taking out a large bundle.*) That's from Paoli of Corsica, that from the Marquis of Squilachi.—Have you a mind to see a letter from Count Poniatowski, now King of Poland—Honest Pon——

[*Searching.*

O, sir, what are you here too? I'll tell you what, honest friend, if you have not absolutely delivered my letter to Sir William Honeywood, you may return it. The thing will do without him.

SIR WILL. Sir, I have delivered it, and must inform you it was received with the most mortifying contempt.

CROAKER. Contempt! My Lofty, what can that mean?

LOFTY. Let him go on, let him go on, I say. You'll find it come to something presently.

SIR WILL. Yes, sir, I believe you'll be amazed, if, after waiting some time in the ante-chamber, after being surveyed with insolent curiosity by the passing servants, I was at last assured, that Sir William Honeywood knew no such person, and I must certainly have been imposed upon.

LOFTY. Good; let me die, very good. Ha! ha! ha!

CROAKER. Now, for my life, I can't find out half the goodness of it.

LOFTY. You can't? Ha! ha!

CROAKER. No, for the soul of me; I think it was as confounded a bad answer as ever was sent from one private gentleman to another.

LOFTY. And so you can't find out the force of the message? Why I was in the house at that very time. Ha! ha! It was I that sent that very answer to my own letter. Ha! ha!

CROAKER. Indeed! How! why!

LOFTY. In one word, things between Sir William and me must be behind the curtain. A party has many eyes. He sides with Lord Buzzard, I side with Sir Gilbert Goose. So that unriddles the mystery.

CROAKER. And so it does indeed, and all my suspicions are over.

LOFTY. Your suspicions! What then, you have been suspecting, you have been suspecting, have you? Mr Croaker, you and I were friends, we are friends no longer. Never talk to me. It's over; I say, it's over!

CROAKER. As I hope for your favour, I did not mean to offend. It escaped me. Don't be discomposed.

LOFTY. Zounds, sir, but I am discomposed, and will be discomposed. To be treated thus! Who am I? Was it for this I have been dreaded both by ins and outs? Have I been libelled in the Gazetteer, and praised in the St James's; have I been chaired at Wildman's, and a speaker at Merchant Tailor's Hall; have I had my hand to addresses, and my head in the print-shops, and talk to me of suspects!

CROAKER. My dear sir, be pacified. What can you have but asking pardon?

LOFTY. Sir, I will not be pacified—Suspects! Who am I? To be used thus, have I paid court to men in favour to serve my friends, the Lords of the Treasury. Sir William Honeywood, and the rest of the gang, and talk to me of suspects! Who am I, I say, who am I?

SIR WILL. Since, sir, you're so pressing for an answer, I'll tell you who you are. A gentleman, as well acquainted with politics, as with men in power; as well acquainted with persons of fashion, as with modesty; with Lords of the Treasury, as with truth; and with all, as you are with Sir William Honeywood. I am Sir William Honeywood!

[*Discovering his ensigns of the Bath.*

CROAKER. Sir William Honeywood!

HONEYW. Astonishment! my uncle! (*Aside.*)

LOFTY. So then my confounded genius has been all this time only leading me up to the garret, in order to fling me out of the window.

CROAKER. What, Mr Importance, and are these your works? Suspect you! You, who have been dreaded by the ins and outs: you, who have had your hand to addresses, and your head stuck up in print-shops. If you were served right, you should have your head stuck up in the pillory.

LOFTY. Ay, stick it where you will, for, by the Lord, it cuts but a very poor figure where it sticks at present.

SIR WILL. Well, Mr Croaker, I hope you now see how incapable this gentleman is of serving you, and how little Miss Richland has to expect from his influence.

CROAKER. Ay, sir, too well I see it, and I can't but say I have had some boding of it these ten days. So I'm resolved, since my son has placed his affections on a lady of moderate fortune to be satisfied with his choice, and not run the hazard of another Mr Lofty, in helping him to a better.

SIR WILL. I approve your resolution, and here they come, to receive a confirmation of your pardon and consent.

Enter MRS CROAKER, JARVIS, LEONTINE, OLIVIA.

MRS CROAKER. Where's my husband? Come, come, lovey, you must forgive them. Jarvis here has been to tell me the whole affair; and, I say, you must forgive them. Our own was a stolen match, you know, my dear; and we never had any reason to repent of it.

CROAKER. I wish we could both say so; however, this gentleman, Sir William Honeywood, has been beforehand with you, in obtaining their pardon. So, if the two poor fools have a mind to marry, I think we can tack them together without crossing the Tweed for it.   [*Joining their hands.*

LEONT. How blest, and unexpected! What, what can we say to such goodness! But our future obedience shall be the best reply. And, as for this gentleman, to whom we owe—

SIR WILL. Excuse me, sir, if I interrupt your thanks, as I have here an interest that calls me. (*Turning to Honeywood.*) Yes, sir, you are surprised to see me; and I own that a desire of correcting your follies led me hither. I saw, with indignation, the errors of a mind that only sought applause from others; that easiness of disposition, which, though inclined to the right, had not courage to condemn the wrong. I saw with regret those splendid errors, that still took name from some neighbouring duty. Your charity, that was but injustice; your benevolence, that was but weakness; and your friendship but credulity. I saw, with regret, great talents and extensive learning only employed to add sprightliness to error, and increase your perplexities. I saw your mind with a thousand natural charms; but the greatness of its beauty served only to heighten my pity for its prostitution.

HONEYW. Cease to upbraid me, sir; I have for some time but too strongly felt the justice of your reproaches. But there is one way still left me. Yes, sir, I have determined, this very hour, to quit forever a place where I have made myself the voluntary slave of all; and to seek among strangers that fortitude which may give strength to the mind, and marshal all its dissipated virtues. Yet, ere I depart, permit me to solicit favour for this gentleman; who, notwithstanding what has happened, has laid me under the most signal obligations. Mr Lofty—

LOFTY. Mr Honeywood, I'm resolved upon a reformation, as well as you. I now begin to find that the man who first invented the art of speaking truth was a much cunninger fellow than I thought him. And to prove that I design to speak truth for the future, I must now assure you that you owe your late enlargement to another; as, upon my soul, I had no hand in the matter. So now, if any of the company has a mind for preferment, he may take my place. I'm determined to resign.   [*Exit.*

HONEYW. How have I been deceived!

SIR WILL. No, sir, you have been obliged to a kinder, fairer friend for that favour. To Miss Richland. Would she complete our joy, and make the man she has honoured by her friendship happy in her love, I should then forget all, and be as blest as the welfare of my dearest kinsman can make me.

MISS RICH. After what is past, it would be but affectation to pretend to indifference. Yes, I will own an attachment, which, I find, was more than friendship. And if my entreaties cannot alter his resolution to quit the country, I will even try if my hand has not power to detain him.

[*Giving her hand.*

HONEYW. Heavens! how can I have deserved all this? How express my happiness, my gratitude? A moment like this over-pays an age of apprehension!

CROAKER. Well, now I see content in every face; but Heaven send we be all better this day three months.

SIR WILL. Henceforth, nephew, learn to respect yourself. He who seeks only for applause from without, has all his happiness in another's keeping.

HONEYW. Yes, sir, I now too plainly perceive my errors. My vanity, in attempting to please all, by fearing to offend any. My meanness in approving folly, lest fools should disapprove. Henceforth, therefore, it shall be my study to reserve my pity for real distress; my friendship for true merit, and my love for her, who first taught me what it is to be happy.

EPILOGUE

SPOKEN BY MRS BULKLEY

As puffing quacks some caitiff wretch procure
To swear the pill, or drop, has wrought a cure:
Thus on the stage, our playwrights still depend
For Epilogues and Prologues on some friend,
Who knows each art of coaxing up the town,
And makes full many a bitter pill go down.
Conscious of this, our bard has gone about,
And teas'd each rhyming friend to help him out.
An Epilogue, things can't go on without it;
It could not fail, would you but set about it.
Young man, cries one (a bard laid up in clover)
Alas, young man, my writing days are over;
Let boys play tricks, and kick the straw, not I;
Your brother Doctor there, perhaps may try.

What I! dear sir, the Doctor interposes,
What, plant my thistle, sir, among his roses?
No, no, I've other contests to maintain;
To-night I head our troops at Warwick Lane.
Go, ask your manager—Who, me? your pardon;
Those things are not our forte at Covent Garden.
Our Author's friends, thus plac'd at happy distance,
Give him good words indeed, but no assistance.
As some unhappy wight, at some new play,
At the Pit door stands elbowing away,
While oft, with many a smile, and many a shrug,
He eyes the centre, where his friends sit snug,
His simpering friends with pleasure in their eyes,
Sink as he sinks, and as he rises rise:
He nods, they nod; he cringes, they grimace;
But not a soul will budge to give him place.
Since then, unhelp'd, our bard must now conform
To 'bide the pelting of this pitiless storm,
Blame where you must, be candid where you can,
And be each critic the Good-Natur'd Man.

www.ingramcontent.com/pod-product-compliance
Ingram Content Group UK Ltd.
Pitfield, Milton Keynes, MK11 3LW, UK
UKHW042147280225
455719UK00001B/168